INTERGROUP
RELATIONS

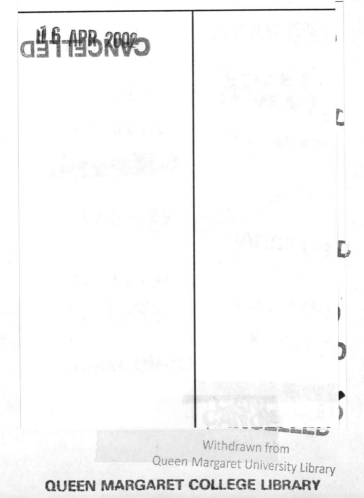

MAPPING SOCIAL PSYCHOLOGY
Series Editor: Tony Manstead

INTERGROUP RELATIONS

Marilynn B. Brewer
and
Norman Miller

OPEN UNIVERSITY PRESS
BUCKINGHAM

Open University Press
Celtic Court
22 Ballmoor
Buckingham
MK18 1XW

First Published 1996

A catalogue record of this book is available from the British Library

ISBN 0 335 09260 8 (pb)   0 335 09261 6 (hb)

Typeset by Graphicraft Typesetters, Hong Kong
Printed in Great Britain by St Edmundsbury Press,
Bury St Edmunds, Suffolk

To Donald T. Campbell,
our uncommon common mentor . . .

CONTENTS

FOREWORD

There has long been a need for a carefully tailored series of reasonably short and inexpensive books on major topics in social psychology, written primarily for students, by authors who enjoy a reputation for the excellence of their research and their ability to communicate clearly and comprehensibly their knowledge of, and enthusiasm for, the discipline. The *Mapping Social Psychology* series has been designed to meet that need. The aim of each volume in the series is to provide a concise and up-to-date overview of the concepts, theories, methods and findings relating to a key topic in social psychology. Although the intention is to produce books that will be used by senior-level undergraduates and graduate students, the fact that the books are written in a straightforward style should also make them accessible to newcomers to social psychology. At the same time, the books are intended to be sufficiently informative and up-to-date to earn the respect of researchers and instructors.

The rationale for this series is twofold. First, conventional textbooks are too low-level and uninformative for use with senior undergraduates or graduate students. Books in this series address this problem partly by dealing with key topics at book length, rather than chapter length, and partly by the fact that each book is authored by an acknowledged expert on the topic in question. Second, traditional textbooks are often dependent on research conducted in, or examples drawn from, North American society. This fosters the mistaken impression that social psychology is an exclusively North American discipline, and can also be baffling for readers who are unfamiliar with North American culture. To combat this problem, authors of books in this series have been encouraged to adopt a broader perspective, citing examples and research from outside North America wherever this is appropriate. The aim is to produce a series for a world market, introducing readers to an international discipline.

The claim that intergroup relations is a topic of key societal importance hardly needs much by way of supportive evidence. Anyone who views the television news receives daily bulletins reporting on the continuation or exacerbation of existing intergroup hostilities, on the development of new crises between ethnic or national groups, or (all too infrequently, it seems) on progress in the solution of some deep-grained conflict between social groups. Understanding the determinants of intergroup conflict is a prime task for social psychologists, as is the search for effective ways of managing and reducing such conflict.

In this latest addition to the *Mapping Social Psychology* series, Marilynn Brewer and Norman Miller provide us with a superb integration of the large and diverse literature on this topic. The book opens with an introduction to a range of concepts (e.g., categorization, accentuation, salience, attribution, social identity, deprivation) used by social psychologists to explain intergroup behavior. Chapter 2 examines the issue of belonging to a group and feeling positive about that group. Members of a group tend to distance themselves from outgroups and feel less positive about those groups, and Chapter 3 explores such outgroup prejudice and hostility. In Chapter 4 the authors consider ingroups and outgroups together, in terms of the pivotal issue of intergroup discrimination: 'normal' considerations of fairness and equality seem to be cast aside when intergroup perceptions and behaviors are involved. The intention is that by gaining an understanding of prejudice, discrimination and conflict, social psychologists can specify ways under which intergroup relations can be improved. Chapter 5 describes what social psychologists have learned about the improvement of intergroup relations. Intergroup relations find their most terrible expression in war, a topic that is not often directly discussed by social psychologists. In their final chapter, Brewer and Miller provide an exciting social psychological analysis, drawing on the preceding chapters, of how international relations can escalate into war.

The quality of this book will come as no surprise to those who are familiar with social psychology in general and with this field of research in particular, given the high standing of the authors in the discipline and the importance of their previous contributions to theory and research on this specific topic. Their book is consistently interesting and enjoyably easy to read. As well as being up-to-date in its coverage, the book does not seek to promote any particular theoretical perspective, making it an ideal introduction to the field. It also manages to draw into a coherent whole relevant material from several fields, ranging from social cognition and social influence, to group processes and political science. As a result, this book considers the issue of intergroup relations at every level of analysis, from the consequences of perceptual categorization by an individual, to the conduct of war between nations. In short, this is a first-class overview of one of the most exciting and socially relevant research topics in social psychology. It will be an excellent resource for students, researchers, and teachers alike.

Tony Manstead
Series Editor

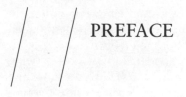

PREFACE

During the 1960s and 70s, the study of intergroup relations had a relatively low profile in social psychology – and in the social sciences more generally. The era of the cold war focused attention on relations between the two political superpowers in the world, and other forms of regional, religious, and ethnic intergroup conflict were either ignored or believed to be largely resolved.

By 1990 this complacency had been shattered. The demise of the Soviet Union and the apparent resurgence of ethnic conflicts throughout the world gave rise to the idea that local group loyalties and intergroup hostilities were never far below the surface. The media began talking about the "new tribalism" that seemed to be emerging everywhere. In one article on the resurgence of ethnic conflict, a journalist from *Time* had the following to say:

> An epidemic of ethnic hatred is sweeping the world, dismaying and perplexing fair-minded people who are at a loss to explain it . . . *Social scientists are not much help with such questions.* They generally regard ethnocentrism – a preference for one's own group – as an innate human characteristic, and they have produced little significant research on the virulent course these feelings often take.
>
> ("An outbreak of bigotry," *Time*, May 28, 1990: 35;
> italics added)

We hope that this book will help prove that statement wrong. Social psychology, in particular, has a great deal to contribute to our understanding of the "virulent course" of intergroup behavior. Even when the focus of theory and research has not been on the study of intergroup relations directly, social psychology's goal of understanding the links between individuals and social groups has produced a wealth of knowledge about the cognitive and motivational underpinnings of perceptions, attitudes, and behaviors toward one's own and other groups. The purpose of this volume is to review and highlight those contributions from social psychological research.

The essence of the social psychological approach to the study of intergroup relations is to understand the causes and consequences of the distinction between *ingroups* (those groups to which an individual belongs) and *outgroups* (social groups that do not include the individual as a member) – the apparently universal propensity to differentiate the social world into "us" and "them." In organizing our presentation of relevant research and theory, we have decomposed intergroup relations into three related but conceptually independent constituent elements. First we discuss the psychological needs and motives associated with individuals' attachment and loyalty to ingroups. Then we turn attention to attitudes and emotions directed toward outgroups. Finally, we look at the comparisons between ingroups and outgroups that lead to discrimination and conflict.

Ultimately, it is our hope that this perspective on the causes and consequences of ingroup–outgroup differentiation will help us not only understand why intergroup relations can become so volatile but also provide insights on how to reduce and prevent the negative manifestations of intergroup distinctions while preserving the values of group loyalty and community.

Acknowledgments

During the course of writing this book we have benefitted greatly from ongoing discussions with colleagues and students who have committed much of their intellectual energy toward enhancing social psychology's contribution to understanding and solving problems of intergroup relations. We are particularly indebted to our own graduate students and participants in our graduate seminars who have helped shape and clarify our conceptual perspective.

More directly, we are enormously grateful to Tony Manstead, editor of the "Mapping Social Psychology" series, who both conceived of this project and saw it through to completion. His patience and support throughout the inordinately long period it took to write this book were essential to making it happen. We also owe tremendous thanks to Sam Gaertner and Michael Hogg, who read and reviewed a complete earlier manuscript of this book and whose comments, suggestions, and encouragement contributed greatly to its improvement. Thanks are due also to Michele Mengali, Valerie Benveniste, and Kim Weaver, who helped with various stages of preparation of the manuscript – often stepping in on short notice to meet looming deadlines.

1 / FROM BASIC PSYCHOLOGICAL PROCESSES TO INTERGROUP CONFLICT

It is a basic fact of human existence that people are organized into social groups. We are all members of many different types of groups, ranging from small, face-to-face groupings of family and friends, to large social categories such as gender, religion, and nationality. As a consequence, a great deal of our interactions with others take place in a group setting, where we are not only individual persons but representatives of our respective social groups. The purpose of this book is to review our knowledge about how social interactions are affected by this group context. In this first chapter we set the stage by presenting essential conceptual ingredients for later chapters and by giving our general perspective on what it means to talk about the "social psychology" of intergroup relations.

Social psychology is unique among the subdisciplines of psychology in dealing with three different levels of analysis – the individual, the interpersonal, and the group. Many of the concepts and ideas that are fundamental in social psychological theory appear at all three levels. Social cognition is the study of how individuals process information about themselves and other individual persons, but it is also about the perceptions that guide interpersonal exchanges, and about cognitive representations of social groups. Social motivations include personal achievement and enhancing individual self-esteem, but also interpersonal attraction and cooperation, and group loyalty and status. Our goal in this book is to describe how cognition and motivation at the individual, interpersonal, and group levels interact and combine to determine intergroup behavior.

What are intergroup relations?

The study of intergroup relations is part of the broader field of social relations. It is concerned with what goes on between humans when social category distinctions exist or are salient. Within the general domain of social psychology, it is a much broader and more complex topic than many others. Understanding intergroup relations invokes virtually every area of social psychological inquiry – from the study of person perception, social attitudes, aggression, self-esteem, social comparison, equity, cooperation and competition, to conformity and compliance. From research in all of these areas we have a wealth of information about the cognitive and motivational underpinnings of intergroup perception and behavior.

In a sense, then, the study of intergroup relations is applied social psychology. It concerns the bearing of specific and more fundamental domains of social psychological knowledge on a particular context – a situation in which there is more than one group. Consequently, the knowledge and principles that have developed within each of these more basic areas need to be considered and applied in terms of their relevance to intergroup relations. At the same time, science seeks to be analytical, which means that complex behaviors must be broken down into their distinct conceptual components. Therefore, as mentioned, this chapter will identify basic distinctions and key processes. Later, in subsequent chapters, we will discuss each of them in more detail, examining in particular their application to group settings.

Defining intergroup settings

First, however, we discuss some preliminary issues. What do we mean by an intergroup setting? For social psychologists, the classic definition of intergroup situations is that provided by Sherif (1966a: 12): "Whenever individuals belonging to one group interact, collectively or individually, with another group or its members *in terms of their group identification*, we have an instance of intergroup behavior."

What this definition implies is that intergroup relations can occur at the level of two persons interacting (the dyadic level) as well as the level of exchanges between groups as a whole (the intergroup level). When Jones, a white male in the personnel department of a company, interviews Smith, a black male who is applying for a job, the interaction is dyadic and at an interpersonal level. Nevertheless, intergroup relations come into play because the social categories of the two actors are manifestly different and likely to affect their interaction. In cross-racial interactions majority members are more uncomfortable and awkward (Henley 1977; Ickes 1984). They exhibit more avoidant nonverbal behaviors, such as less eye contact, and other symptoms of anxiety such as speech errors (Crosby et al. 1980). At the same time, the minority group member is likely to be suspicious and distrustful of the majority member (Crocker and Major 1989; Feagin 1992), see him as prejudiced (Crocker et al. 1991), and be less communicative (Berg and Wright-Buckley 1988).

When personnel officer Jones examined Mr Smith's application file prior to inviting him in for an interview, intergroup relations were represented symbolically rather than behaviorally. At that stage there was no actual exchange between Jones and Smith, but nevertheless, the fact that Smith's social category differed from that of Jones was likely to affect Jones's thoughts and evaluations, again making the situation a part of the more general arena covered by intergroup relations. Jones's beliefs (stereotypes) about, and affect (attitude) toward the social category, African-American, will distort not only his evaluation of Smith's attributes or job qualifications (Jussim et al. 1987), but also his inferences or explanations (attributions) for why Smith has the positive and the negative qualities evident in the file (Hewstone 1990), and his predictions for Smith's future behavior (Jackson et al. 1993).

This same distinction between face-to-face interaction and symbolic representation applies to nondyadic intergroup settings in which multiple persons of each social category are present. Members of the 16-person school board of governors may organize themselves into competing factions when discussing how to distribute monies throughout the district. The racial/ethnic identities of the various board members may cause them to act as distinct groups, each representing their own ethnic constituency in their face-to-face bargaining. On the other hand, when the three males who comprise the executive committee of the personnel department meet to discuss company policy for leaves of absence, members of the social category "female" are not present. Nevertheless, females may be a symbolically represented category made salient because of recent media attention to the potential need of female workers for maternity leaves. Finally, some groups contain so many members that the possibility of simultaneous face-to-face interaction between their respective members is impossible. In such instances, a representative of each may interact, as when the leader of each of two nation-states that are in conflict meet to discuss an issue of contention. Though the interaction is dyadic, each category is symbolically present as a whole.

Intergroup settings, then, can include dyadic interactions or group interactions where group members are actually physically present or symbolically present.

What behavior is studied in intergroup research?

In the most general sense, two kinds of responses toward a group or one of its members are potentially available: prosocial behavior and antisocial behavior. Although both positive and negative interactions are studied in the realm of interpersonal relationships, intergroup relations are most often seen as fraught with tension, conflict, and antagonism. Indeed, the study of intergroup relations has become synomous with the study of intergroup conflict.

The most salient cases of intergroup behavior in the real world often consist of violent acts, such as the shooting of a rival gang member, or the deaths incurred by war. Statistically, most instances of assault, violence, and aggression occur within, not between, groups. Nevertheless, acts of intergroup aggression are more newsworthy, perhaps in part because they have the potential to escalate into more widespread violence. In fact, there is evidence that intergroup aggression is perceived as more violent and severe than acts of interpersonal aggression (Otten et al. 1995).

Although escalation of conflict and hostility between groups is the form of intergroup relationships of most concern in the real world, social psychological research on intergroup behavior starts with other, more subtle, forms of responding that reflect differences in *disposition* toward others as a function of their group membership. In general, feelings, beliefs, and interpersonal behaviors tend to be more positive when they involve members of the same group than when they occur between groups. As we shall see in later chapters, it is not just that individuals are more negative in their attitudes and behaviors toward outgroup members, but also that prosocial behaviors such as helping and cooperation are more likely to be extended to members of the ingroup and withheld from the outgroup. Understanding how basic perceptions, affect, and motives are influenced or transformed by an intergroup setting is the essence of the social psychological approach to the study of intergroup relations.

Building blocks for the study of intergroup relations

We turn now to the separate ingredients or building blocks that need to be considered in understanding intergroup relations from a social psychological perspective. These basic processes come from research on *social cognition, social comparison,* and *social motives*; we provide a brief overview of each of these in the following sections.

Social cognition: categorization

Perhaps the most basic process of human judgment and cognition is that of categorization – the lumping together of objects and events into meaningful groupings that enables a person to deal with incoming information quickly and automatically. Categorization is a natural product of how the human mind operates and is fundamental to the study of intergroup relations in that it is the basis upon which groups are identified in the first place.

In his now classic analysis of the nature of prejudice, Allport (1954) notes five important characteristics of categorization:

1 it forms large classes and clusters for guiding our daily adjustments;
2 categorization assimilates as much as it can to the cluster;
3 the category enables us to quickly identify a related object;
4 the category saturates all that it contains with the same ideational and emotional flavor – that is, the same affect is elicited by all instances of the category;
5 categories are rational in that they are based on existing differences between characteristics of objects classified into separate categories.

These features identified by Allport hold for both social and nonsocial categorizations. Social categories, however, have a special feature that is not associated with categorizations of objects or events outside of the social domain. Individuals themselves are members of social categories. Thus, the act of categorizing a person into a social grouping automatically classifies that individual as a member of an *ingroup* (a category to which the perceiver belongs) or an *outgroup* (a category to which the perceiver does not belong). It is perhaps for this reason that Allport felt that social categories tend to be less rational than other categorizations in that the beliefs we hold about social groupings often do not rest on firm evidence of actual intergroup differences.

Researchers in cognitive psychology have distinguished between natural categories (e.g. animals, plants) and social categories (e.g. political parties, ethnic groups). Natural categories are thought to have essential characteristics that account for why one sees specific instances of the category as similar – as sharing the "essence" of the category (Medin 1989). Some social categories, such as ethnicity, eventually come to be seen as "naturalized," as sharing an essence as do natural categories (Rothbart and Taylor 1992).

Most researchers assume that this tendency to see some social categories as equivalent to natural categories is culturally learned. Others, however, point to evidence that the human has distinct cognitive competences (e.g. Cheng and Holyoak 1985) and that the infant and young child have predispositions for certain types of information and tasks (Gelman 1988; Gelman and Wellman 1991). Building on these domain-specific predispositions and cognitive capacities, they argue that such domain-specificity extends to social categories. By contrast to other social categories such as political parties, race/ethnicity does not become similar to natural categories as a result of cultural learning, but instead, is a domain for which infants have a predisposition for categorization (Hirschfield 1988). Regardless of which explanation is correct, social categories that have some biological basis, such as those based on gender or ethnic inheritance, have acquired a special status in the study of intergroup relations.

Category accentuation

One feature of categorization processes that was not discussed by Allport is especially important to an understanding of intergroup perceptions. Although categories may be based initially on actual differences among objects, once categories have been formed there is a tendency for perceivers to exaggerate the extent of differences between members of one category and another. This category accentuation is a consequence of processes of assimilation and contrast whereby we judge items within the same category as more similar (assimilation) and items from different categories as more dissimilar (contrast) than they actually are (Tajfel 1969). The result is an increase in perceived homogeneity within categories and distinctiveness between categories.

A concrete demonstration of category accentuation was provided in a judgment experiment by Tajfel and Wilkes (1963). The stimuli in that experiment were eight lines, varying in length from 16.2cm to 22.9cm. For some judges, the lines were presented without labels. For others, the four shorter lines were labeled with the letter A and the four longer lines were labeled B. Judges were shown the lines, one at a time in random order, and asked to estimate the length of each. The average estimates produced by judges in the categorization (label) condition, compared to those in the no-label condition, exaggerated the difference in length between lines labeled A and lines labeled B. This effect was particularly marked for the two lines at the boundary of the categories. The difference between the perceived length of the longest line in category A and the shortest line in category B was much greater than the actual difference between the two lines. As a result, the perceived distinctiveness of the two categories was accentuated. Similar effects are obtained when people judge heights of men and women (Biernat et al. 1991). On average, men are taller than women, but this difference is exaggerated when judges make estimates of the heights of individual males and females.

By the same process, members of a social group are perceived to have similar attitudes and to be different from members of other groups, even when the group assignments have been arbitrary (Wilder 1981). In general, the more salient category distinctions are, the less we notice individual differences within categories and the more we see each group as a single, homogeneous unit. Once categories have been formed, we are biased toward information that enhances the differences between categories and less attentive to information about similarities between members of different categories (Krueger et al. 1989). These effects of categorization are now widely recognized as the psychological foundation for social stereotyping and intergroup prejudice (Tajfel 1969; Hamilton and Trolier 1986; Wilder 1986a; Hewstone et al. 1991).

Category salience

Within the social domain, the most fundamental category distinctions are those that differentiate ingroups from outgroups. As we shall see in subsequent chapters, this ingroup–outgroup distinction – and the consequent accentuation of differences between ingroup categories and others – is the fundamental component of social psychological theories of intergroup relations. Thus, in order to understand the dynamics of intergroup behavior, we must first understand what bases of social categorization are used to draw these important ingroup–outgroup differentiations.

As we mentioned above, the relevance and salience of any particular social categorization may be context-specific. Some category memberships may be highly meaningful in one social situation (e.g. the difference between psychologists and sociologists at an academic conference) and irrelevant in others (e.g. a social reception for foreign dignitaries). Bruner (1957) hypothesized that the likelihood of using a particular categorization was determined in part by what the perceiver expected to see and in part by the nature of the stimulus objects or events in the environment. More specifically, Bruner stated that the salience of any particular category distinction would be determined by the interaction between category accessibility (the frequency or importance of that categorization to the perceiver) and fit (the match between category specifications and the current stimuli).

Applying Bruner's model to the categorization of people in social groups, Oakes and colleagues (1991; also Oakes *et al.* 1994) have suggested that the perceived "fit" for social categories has two aspects. The first is *comparative fit* – the extent to which differences within categories are less than differences between categories among the persons in a particular context. The second is *normative fit* – the extent to which the specific persons match expectations about category differences. For instance, in a group of six persons containing three females and three males, gender is likely to be an accessible and salient categorization. In most cases, physical features, appearance, and dress will be more similar within gender than between. However, if all members of our six-person group have short hair, are wearing jeans and flannel shirts, and talking about football, gender will not be a salient categorization because neither the comparative fit (differentiation between categories) nor normative fit (match to expected gender differences) are high.

An experimental study by van Knippenberg and colleagues (1994) confirmed the importance of normative fit in determining whether a particular category distinction becomes salient. Participants viewed a videotape of a discussion group among male and female students and teachers. Results of a later test of participants' memory for material on the videotape indicated that categorization by gender was greater when the topic of the discussion was gender-related (i.e. the merits of positive discrimination in favor of women) rather than unrelated (e.g. preventing welfare fraud), particularly when the positions taken by the males and females on the tape were consistent with gender expectations.

Cross-categorization

Much of the social psychological research on intergroup relations has been conducted in settings in which one, and only one, ingroup–outgroup category distinction is highly salient or dominant. But in a pluralistic society, individuals simultaneously hold memberships in multiple social categories. Within the same setting, a particular person might be identified in terms of gender, ethnicity, political party affiliation, religion, or occupation. Any two persons in that situation may share membership in some of those categories, but belong to different categories on others. When two or more category distinctions are available, the implications for how ingroup–outgroup differentiations are drawn are not always clear.

Circumstances in which more than one social categorization may be salient, and where persons share category membership on one dimension but not another, have been defined as instances of *crossed categorization* (Deschamps and Doise 1978; Hewstone *et al.* 1993). The interesting question in situations of cross-categorization is what happens to ingroup–outgroup distinctions when more than one categorization is available? One possible effect of crossed category distinctions would be to dilute the meaningfulness of any ingroup–outgroup differentiation and eliminate category accentuation effects. In this case, ingroup–outgroup differences would be reduced or eliminated and perceptions of others would be equivalent, regardless of category membership. Such canceling effects have been demonstrated in experiments by Deschamps and Doise (1978) and Vanbeselaere (1987).

A second possibility is that the two category distinctions are additive in their effects, so that shared membership on either dimension provides some basis for ingroup differentiation. Alternatively, the two dimensions may be additive, but one is more important or dominant. Such additive patterns have been observed in a number of studies involving combinations of gender, ethnicity, and religious categories (Brewer *et al.* 1987; Hagendoorn and Henke 1991; Hewstone *et al.* 1993).

Finally, individuals might be especially sensitive to any form of ingroup or outgroup differentiation, regardless of the dimension of categorization. Sometimes we are attentive to any information that indicates similarity between ourselves and others; at other times we are tuned to information about dissimilarity. If individuals are looking for similarity, shared ingroup membership will be what matters. In that case, only a "double outgroup" will be perceived as an outgroup (Brown and Turner 1979). On the other hand, if cues to dissimilarity are salient, the individual will be more sensitive to nonshared categories. In this case, outgroup distinctions of any kind may dominate: only the "double ingroup" will be perceived as an ingroup, all others categorized as an outgroup (Schofield and Sagar 1977; Eurich-Fulcer and Schofield 1995). In later chapters we will consider the conditions under which individuals might be especially sensitive to ingroup versus outgroup classifications in defining any intergroup situation.

Social cognition: attribution

It is a basic tenet of social cognition research that people find it unpleasant to be in a state of uncertainty. They actively seek to explain and interpret the causes of events and experiences. Further, the explanations that they come up with have a major impact on how they react – both emotionally and behaviorally – to events. Attribution theory is that branch of social cognition research that deals with how people perceive the causes of social events and of their own and others' behavior.

Theory and research on causal attribution owes a major debt to Fritz Heider, who attempted to account for how the untrained observer or naïve psychologist makes sense out of, or accounts for, why another person behaved as she did (Heider 1944, 1958). Heider provided several key ideas that were important to subsequent research and theorizing about attributional processes.

First, Heider emphasized that the naïve perceiver does not assimilate information objectively. In developing an account for another person's action, it is not just the action itself that is important, but how that action is understood by the observer. Thus, the observer's emotional reaction to the behavior, as well as the beliefs that the observer holds about the other person, will affect how the action is interpreted and how the observer explains the behavior.

Heider's second important contribution was the distinction between the person versus the situation as potential causes of a particular behavior. When trying to account for the reasons a behavior occurred, we can either look to factors internal to the person or to factors in the external environment. Heider noted that we tend to ignore or underestimate the importance of situational determinants of behavior and emphasize instead internal attributes of the behaving person.

In discussing this bias, Heider used the phrase, "behavior engulfs the field." What he meant was that the array of situational influences in the environment in which the actor is located (the "field") is obscured or masked by the salience of the behavior being observed and its natural link to the person generating that behavior. In the eye of the observer, a behavior is not seen as separate from the actor. Thus it is easy or automatic to see behavior as a product of some characteristic or trait of the person. This tendency to interpret or explain an action in terms of the actor's character, personality, or traits, and to underestimate the influence of situational factors in prompting that action has been termed the *fundamental attribution error* (Ross 1977).

Causal explanations for events and behaviors can differ in other ways besides whether they are internal or external to the person. For instance, both ability and effort are internal factors, but ability is typically thought to be a stable characteristic of the individual whereas the amount of effort an individual makes can change from one situation to another. The *locus* of a cause refers to the person–situation distinction whereas *stability* refers to the temporal nature of a cause. A stable cause is one that involves a persistent characteristic, invariably present over time, as opposed to a factor that is variable, sometimes present and other times not.

A third important distinction among causal attributions is that of *controllability*, the degree to which the cause is something that can be determined by volition or intent. Ability as an explanation of good performance is an internal, stable attribution, but to the extent that it is based on heritable characteristics, it is one that is uncontrollable. Effort, in contrast, is unstable but under control of the actor, and is thus both unstable and controllable. Controllability is related to perceived responsibility for actions, and underlies the distinction between excuses and justification for negative behaviors (Weiner *et al.* 1987). A justification does not deny that one is responsible for the behavior, but it does undermine the negative evaluation of that behavior. In contrast, an excuse acknowledges that the behavior may have been bad or morally wrong, but diminishes or denies one's responsibility for having engaged in it.

These three general dimensions of causal attributions – locus, stability, and controllability – constitute a basic taxonomy of social attributions (Weiner 1985, 1986). More importantly, they influence how we respond to another person's actions. When we perceive a behavior as caused by internal, stable attributes of the person being observed, we react differently than if the behavior is seen as externally caused or unstable. For instance, if the individual ahead of you in a queue steps on your foot, you will feel angry (and perhaps retaliate) if you believe it was a controllable act of hostility; but if you interpret it as an uncontrollable accident caused by crowding, you are likely to respond quite differently. In the case of violent behaviors, excuses may produce less escalation of conflict than might justifications.

Since attributions have implications for how we treat another person, and since attributions are subjective judgments, understanding attributional processes is one key to understanding intergroup behavior. This is particularly true if the attributions we make about another individual's actions are influenced by group membership, as indicated by results of research on attributional biases.

Biases in attribution
We have previously discussed the internal/external dimension and the fundamental attribution error. Research has revealed another type of attributional bias which operates within the context of the fundamental attribution error. Even though there is an overall tendency toward explaining events in terms of person attributes, this tendency is stronger when we are making attributions about the causes of *other* people's behavior than when we explain our own actions. We are more likely to see our own behavior as being responsive to the situation – i.e. as having external causes. This is particularly true for negative behaviors or outcomes. When individuals take internal responsibility for good actions but attribute

bad outcomes to unstable or external causes, this is known as a *self-serving* attributional bias.

Self-serving biases appear to extend to intergroup attributions as well. Good outcomes for the ingroup are explained by stable, internal attributions. Bad outcomes for the ingroup are explained by situational factors, or unstable internal attributes. By contrast, good outcomes for the outgroup are explained by situational factors, or by unstable internal factors (e.g. effort or luck). Bad outcomes for the outgroup are explained by stable, internal factors. Pettigrew (1979) termed this pattern of intergroup attributions the "ultimate attribution error." This particular bias serves both to enhance a positive image of the ingroup, compared to outgroups, and to protect the ingroup from the negative implications of bad actions (Hewstone 1990; Weber 1994).

The role of ingroup-enhancing attributional biases in attachment to ingroups is discussed further in Chapter 2. The ingroup protective biases have important implications for the initiation and maintenance of intergroup hostilities, as discussed in Chapter 6. If we attribute a negative action to evil intent or aggression dispositions, we are much more likely to respond with retaliatory violence than if we attribute that same act to a temporary situation (Betancourt and Blair 1992). Actions by ingroup members that are hostile or violent are more likely to be perceived as justified by the situation than are similar actions by outgroup members (Hewstone 1990; Weber 1994). Among the external factors in the situation that account for our behavior is the behavior of the other group. *We* are only responding to *them*. By contrast, in our view of the outgroup, we account for their action in terms of their internal attributes, their natural characteristics – not the situation that we may in part have actually created for them. Whereas we see ourselves as responding to the situation and to them, their behavior is perceived as due to their characteristics and aggressive intent. Thus intergroup attributional biases help to perpetuate conflict because both sides in a conflict can feel justified in continuing aggression.

Social comparison: evaluating self and others

In addition to their need to interpret and explain others' behavior, individuals have a strong need to evaluate their own abilities and characteristics – to know where they stand on various dimensions of behavior or performance (Festinger 1954). Such evaluations are often comparative by nature. Some comparisons are based on changes in the self over time. Children, for instance, often take pride in their growth, marking their height on the back of a door and noting with glee the difference between last year's mark and that achieved this year. The comparison of marks provides a basis for judgment about how much better one is now than before. Similarly, one can mark improvement in skills or in performance in games such as golf by comparison with one's own past performance.

Self-evaluations are more difficult with respect to attributes for which there is no physical or absolute standard. In such instances, judgments about good and bad are based on comparison with others. If one gets a C+ in a class in which most others obtain As and Bs, one may not take much pride from that outcome. Yet, in a class in which the instructor imposes very stringent and perhaps indefensible standards, knowing that one got a C+, and that there were only a few Bs and no As, may be a legitimate source of pride.

There are two important points here. The first is that most judgments are relative rather than absolute, as shown by adaptation level theory (Helson 1964). Any one stimulus is judged against the background of prior stimuli within that domain. A two-gram weight will appear light to the weightlifter, but heavy to someone who repairs watches. Bench-pressing a hundred pounds will be easy (light) for the weightlifter, but heavy for the novice. The second is that for many dimensions of judgment, there is no physical standard against which one can base one's evaluation. In such cases, one must rely on social comparison to other persons or groups. Because judgments about the goodness of one's performance or one's outcomes are often necessarily comparative, there is a sense in which such comparisons are intrinsically competitive. In order to validate a positive perception of myself, it is not enough to be "good" in an absolute sense but to be "better" than others (Wills 1981).

The basic motives of self-evaluation and self-enhancement can be met by actual comparisons between oneself and other persons or groups, or by making certain assumptions about others' attributes. For instance, people often assume that others are similar to themselves in attitudes and beliefs, thereby providing social support for their own view. Such perceived consensus can fulfill self-enhancement motives. For attitudes and many behaviors, what is good and correct is defined by social consensus. Thus the tendency to overestimate consensus with respect to one's own beliefs and actions can contribute to self-worth and self-consistency.

Self-enhancement motivation, however, can also motivate imagined difference rather than consensus. Ordinarily, people are inclined to see themselves as similar to others in their attitudes, but for abilities, uniqueness may be more positive (Marks 1984). A distinctively good ability sets one apart from the pack, and bolsters self-esteem. This may also be the case for attitudinal dimensions that have moral implications, where the good and bad ends of the dimension are clearly discernible. For these types of issues, individuals are more likely to see their own position as unique and dissimilar to others rather than as similar to them.

Social comparison also operates at the intergroup level. The distinctiveness and value of one's own group is derived, at least in part, from comparison to other groups. Comparisons that favor the ingroup enhance group esteem – group members are likely to prefer intergroup situations in which their own group maintains positive distinctiveness and to minimize or resist intergroup comparisons that are not so favorable to the ingroup (Brewer 1979). The consequences of such biased intergroup comparison provide much of the foundation for intergroup discrimination discussed in Chapter 4.

Relative deprivation and perceived justice
Just as abilities and attributes are evaluated by comparison with others, the value attached to outcomes such as economic or social rewards may also be determined by social comparison. The same salary could be a source of satisfaction or dissatisfaction, depending on whether other people are earning more than I am. A great deal of research on social justice supports the idea that individuals' feelings of being deprived or disadvantaged are based on the comparisons they make rather than the absolute value of their own condition. Feelings of resentment and the sense of injustice that arises from perceiving that one has less than is deserved (compared to others) is called *relative deprivation*.

The concept of relative deprivation was developed by social scientists during World War II to explain some paradoxical findings that emerged in the study of morale among American soldiers (Stouffer *et al.* 1949). Researchers found, for instance, that soldiers in air force units, where rates of promotion were quite high, had *more* complaints about the promotion system than did soldiers in the military police, where promotions were few and far between. Equally surprising, they found that black soldiers who were stationed in southern states in the US (where overt discrimination based on race was very visible) had *higher* morale than black soldiers stationed in the less racist northern states. Stouffer and his colleagues explained these anomalous results in terms of different standards of comparison being used by soldiers in different units. Compared to peers who were advancing at a rapid rate, air force soldiers who had not yet been promoted felt deprived, even though their objective chances of promotion were higher than those of soldiers in other units. Similarly, the high morale of black soldiers stationed in the South may have derived from comparisons with black civilians who fared very poorly; black soldiers in the North, on the other hand, may have felt deprived relative to civilian blacks in that region who were earning higher wages in war-related factory jobs.

Relative deprivation may be experienced even by those who are objectively advantaged but feel they are losing by comparison to previous expectations. This principle was dramatically illustrated by the behavior of young members of the upper castes of India in a series of incidents in 1990. During one period that year, scores of middle-class youths (members of the Brahmin, Kshatriya, and Vaishya castes) committed suicide in protest against government policies opening more jobs to the poor. By any objective standards, the upper castes were doing quite well, even in the face of government economic reforms designed to benefit the disadvantaged castes. Yet the perception that their own caste was losing position relative to the lower castes created a sense of comparative disadvantage that was sufficient to motivate dramatic protest against the reforms.

Just as experiences of relative deprivation can occur even among the advantaged, members of disadvantaged groups in general may not feel deprived or aggrieved if they compare themselves to similarly disadvantaged others. Women professionals, for instance, tend to feel satisfied with their jobs, despite lower pay and status, as long as they compare their outcomes with those of other female colleagues and not with male colleagues (Zanna *et al.* 1987).

Since individuals tend to limit their interpersonal social comparisons to members of their own ingroups, does this mean that women and other economically and politically disadvantaged groups never resent their position relative to men or higher status groups? The answer to that question rests on an important distinction between the experience of relative deprivation at the personal level and what Runciman (1966) called *fraternal deprivation*. Fraternal deprivation arises from comparisons between the outcomes of one's ingroup as a whole and those of more advantaged groups. While personal deprivation depends on interpersonal comparisons with similar others, fraternal deprivation involves intergroup comparisons between dissimilar groups. Feelings of personal deprivation and fraternal deprivation are not necessarily closely connected. Indeed, it is frequently found that members of disadvantaged groups perceive that their group is discriminated against but report that they, personally, have not experienced any discrimination (Crosby 1982; Taylor *et al.* 1990). As we will discuss in more detail in Chapter 4, feelings of injustice arising from relative deprivation have very different consequences depending on whether the comparison involves personal or fraternal deprivation (Vanneman and Pettigrew 1972; Walker and Pettigrew 1984).

Social motives: cooperation or competition

Responses to relative deprivation reflect the influence of social motivation. Social motives refer to the value an individual places on outcomes received by the self and others. If a person is interested strictly in the absolute value of outcomes to him or herself, this form of self-interest represents an asocial motive, in the sense that others' outcomes are not taken into account, only one's own. In most situations, however, people do not seem to evaluate their costs and benefits in this absolute sense, but instead value their own outcomes in relation to those obtained by others.

The theory of social motives (McClintock 1972; MacCrimmon and Messick, 1976; McClintock and Liebrand 1988) designates five forms of social motivation that are particularly important in the conduct of human affairs. These motives represent different orientations that an individual can bring to a social interaction; they determine what that individual is seeking to achieve in the interaction and how satisfied he or she will be with the outcomes. The five basic social motives are:

1 Relative gain orientation – seeking to maximize the difference between outcomes to oneself compared to others. This is the

motivational orientation associated with pure competition, where
the value associated with one's own outcomes is determined
by how much they exceed another's outcomes. In a competitive
game such as soccer, for instance, it is not the absolute number
of points that a team scores that counts, only the number more
than that scored by the other team.

2 Joint gain orientation – seeking to maximize the total outcomes
for self and others combined. This is the motivational orientation of pure cooperation. This motivation would be characteristic
of members of a team whose goal is to score as many points
as possible for the group as a whole; it is also the motivation
associated with cooperative partnerships and other ventures in
which the goal is to maximize profits for everyone in the group.

3 Equality – seeking to minimize the difference between one's own
and others' outcomes. This is the social motive that is opposite
to that associated with competition. With this orientation, goals
of fairness and equal distribution of outcomes are primary.

4 Other's gain orientation – seeking to maximize the value of
outcomes to another person, regardless of one's own outcomes.
This is the orientation associated with pure altruism. Altruism
does not necessarily imply that the individual sacrifice in order
to benefit another, but that his or her primary concern is the
welfare of the other person rather than the self. This is the
motivational orientation associated with parental care or other
caregiving relationships.

5 Other's loss orientation – seeking to minimize the outcomes of
another person. In contrast to altruism, this is the social motive
associated with pure aggression, where the individual's primary
goal is to harm the other, regardless of outcomes to the self.

The differences among the five motivational orientations can
be illustrated by considering the array of alternative pairs of outcomes displayed in Figure 1.1. Imagine that the numbers in these
arrays represent the absolute value of psychological and material
outcomes that are achieved by one person (self) and another. The
different pairings of outcomes represent different possible relationships between those achieved by the self compared to the other.
An individual who was purely self-interested would prefer option
A to all of the others because that is the one in which self-gain is
highest, ignoring what outcomes to the other are. An individual
with a relative gain orientation, however, would prefer option B.

Figure 1.1 Assessing social motives

Pairings of outcomes for self and other

	A	B	C	D	E	F
Self	50	40	40	40	20	20
Other	40	20	40	60	70	10

Even though this alternative gives lower outcomes to the self than does option A, it is the one in which the relative difference between self and other is greater in one's own favor. Similarly, someone with an equality orientation would prefer C over A, because equal outcomes are more important than absolute gain.

From the array in Figure 1.1, an individual with a joint gain (cooperative) social orientation would prefer option D over all others because that is the pairing in which the total outcomes to both parties are maximized. An individual with an altruistic orientation would prefer option E, whereas someone who was motivated by aggression would choose option F. These latter preferences are dictated by the value of the outcomes to the other person, ignoring one's own outcomes.

The five social motives defined above represent pure motivational states, where the individual has a single goal that drives preferences within a social interaction. In many situations, of course, an individual will have mixed orientations. For instance, relative gain may be moderated by some concern for equality, so that the individual seeks to be better off than others but not by too wide a margin. Altruism and aggression may be moderated by concern for one's own outcomes, and so forth. To some extent, the social motives that an individual brings to a situation are determined by individual differences in socialization and values – some people are dispositionally competitive across a wide range of social situations; others are dispositionally cooperative (McClintock and Liebrand 1988). But motives can also be influenced by the situation itself. Many games and competitions, for instance, require a relative gain orientation, while other situations of social interdependence require mutual cooperation. Of particular concern to intergroup relations is the distinction between cooperative and competitive social motives. In later chapters we will discuss evidence that individuals are more likely to adopt a cooperative orientation in interactions within their ingroup, but switch to a competitive orientation when the interaction involves outgroup members.

Figure 1.2   The interrelationship of individual and group processes

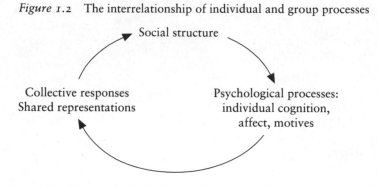

Perspectives on individuals and social groups

Social categorization, causal attribution, social comparison, co-operation and competition are the cognitive and motivational processes on which current social psychological theories of inter-group relations are built. These processes are significantly influenced by the group context in which the individual is operating. In the research reviewed in this chapter we have seen many examples of how cognition, affect, and motivations are influenced by the social structure of the situation – by what social categories are salient and meaningful. But these psychological responses, in turn, shape the behaviors that lead to collective consequences; the social structure of the situation is influenced by the cognitions, affect, and motivations of the individual participants. From the social psychological perspective, the individual and the social group constitute a reciprocal causal system in which cognitions and motivation are the associative links, as represented in Figure 1.2.

In the chapters that follow we will demonstrate how social psychological research and theory have forged these associative links between individual and group processes. We begin with a focus on the cognitive and motivational origins of attachment to one's own social groups – the formation of ingroups. We then move to the psychology of prejudice against outgroups – attitudes and emotions directed toward those who are distinguished from "us." Finally, we focus on the social psychology of differentiation between the ingroup and outgroups, and its consequences for inter-group discrimination and conflict. The last two chapters deal with applications of the social psychological approach toward reducing prejudice and discrimination and understanding the origins of war. Running throughout these chapters is the general theme that individual psychology and group psychology are inextricably intertwined.

Further reading

Allport, G. W. (1954). *The nature of prejudice*. Cambridge, MA: Addison-Wesley. The classic book on social psychological underpinnings of intergroup relations.

Hamilton, D. L. and Trolier, T. (1986). Stereotypes and stereotyping: An overview of the cognitive approach. In J. Dovidio and S. Gaertner (eds) *Prejudice, discrimination and racism*, pp. 127–64. New York: Academic Press. A review of social cognition applied to intergroup perception.

McClintock, C. G. (1972). Social motivation: A set of propositions. *Behavioral Science*, 17, 438–54. A taxonomy of different social motives or orientations to interpersonal exchanges.

Tajfel, H. (1969). Cognitive aspects of prejudice. *Journal of Social Issues*, 25, 79–97. The initial paper on social categorization theory.

2 / ETHNOCENTRISM AND INGROUP IDENTITY: THE NEED FOR "WE-NESS"

On November 18, 1978, more than 900 men, women, and children committed suicide at Jonestown in Guyana. Told that their group was under seige, members of the Reverend Jim Jones's People's Temple lined up to receive glasses of red Kool Aid laced with cyanide. All drank the liquid as they were told, and almost all died within 30 minutes.

The dramatic suicides of members of the Jonestown cult illustrate the extremes to which individuals will go on behalf of the groups to which they belong. Warfare brings out acts of extreme cruelty and of extreme heroism, both in the name of group loyalty. At a more mundane level, many of the things we do make sense only if they are understood as expressions of our identification with a group. Many of our day-to-day choices about what to wear, how to spend leisure time, and what political positions to espouse are influenced by a desire to symbolize or represent our important group memberships. In this chapter we will review research on the formation of group identities and the evidence for the powerful effects of group identification on individual behavior. This will be followed by a discussion of theories about why individuals become attached to social groups and what role this plays in intergroup relations.

Ethnocentrism: the ingroup and the self

The apparently universal tendency for human beings to differentiate themselves according to group membership was documented in rich anthropological observations compiled by Sumner (1906). Sumner adopted the terms *in-group* and *out-group* to refer to social groupings to which a particular individual belongs or does not belong, respectively. Ingroups could be of many different types, ranging from small, face-to-face groupings of family and friends, to large social categories such as gender, religion, and nationality. The psychological meaning of group membership does not seem to be restricted by group size or direct interaction with fellow group members. For some people, national citizenship or social class has as much influence on their behavior as their own immediate family.

Ingroup membership is more than mere cognitive classification – it carries emotional significance as well. Attachment to ingroups and preference of ingroups over outgroups may be a universal characteristic of human social life. Sumner coined the term *ethnocentrism* to refer to this social psychological phenomenon:

> a differentiation arises between ourselves, the we-group, or in-group, and everybody else, or the others-groups, out-groups. The insiders in a we-group are in a relation of peace, order, law, government, and industry, to each other . . . Ethnocentrism is the technical name for this view of things in which one's own group is the center of everything, and all others are scaled and rated with reference to it . . . Each group nourishes its own pride and vanity, boasts itself superior, exalts its own divinities, and looks with contempt on outsiders.
>
> (Sumner 1906: 12–13)

Such group loyalties are apparently acquired early in life. By age six or seven, for instance, children exhibit a strong preference for their own nationality, even before the concept of "nation" has been fully understood (Tajfel *et al.* 1970). Evidence for the pervasiveness of ingroup preference extends beyond the literature on ethnic and national identity. Experimental social psychologists have demonstrated that even classifying individuals into arbitrary categories in the laboratory can elicit ingroup–outgroup feelings (Tajfel *et al.* 1971; Turner 1978; Brewer 1979). And there is experimental evidence that the concepts "we" and "us" carry positive emotional significance that is activated automatically and unconsciously (Perdue *et al.* 1990).

According to Sumner's analysis, the essential characteristics of an individual's relationship to ingroups are loyalty and preference.

Loyalty is represented in adherence to ingroup norms and trust-worthiness in dealings with fellow ingroup members. Preference is represented in differential acceptance of ingroup members over members of outgroups and positive evaluation of ingroup characteristics that differ from those of outgroups. Ethnocentric loyalty and preference are analogous to self-integrity and self-esteem. Ethnocentrism at the group level parallels egocentrism at the individual level (Messick and Mackie 1989).

The comparison between egocentrism and ethnocentrism has been reformulated by social psychologists Henri Tajfel and John Turner in terms of a distinction between personal identity and social identity (Turner 1982; Hogg and Abrams 1988). Personal identity refers to self-conceptualizations that define the individual in relation to (or in comparison to) other individuals. Social identities refer to conceptualizations of the self that derive from membership in emotionally significant social categories or groups (Turner 1985). Tajfel and Turner's distinction between personal and social identity is similar to Harry Triandis's distinction between the private self and the collective self in cross-cultural contexts (Triandis 1989; Trafimow *et al.* 1991). It is also represented in the distinction between individual and collective self-esteem as bases of self-worth (Crocker and Luhtanen 1990; Luhtanen and Crocker 1992).

Although both are aspects of the individual self, personal identity and social identity are mutually exclusive levels of self-definition. Classification of oneself as a group member entails "a shift towards the perception of the self as an interchangeable exemplar of some social category *and away from* the perception of self as a unique person" (Turner *et al.* 1987: 50; italics added). In other words, social identities are categorizations of the self into more inclusive social units that depersonalize the self representation. In this sense, depersonalization does not mean a loss of individual identity, but rather a change from the personal to the social level of identity, with consequent change in the nature and content of salient self-concepts.

When a particular social identity is made salient, individuals are likely to think of themselves as having characteristics that are representative of that social category. Social identity, in other words, leads to *self-stereotyping* (Simon and Hamilton 1994). This effect was demonstrated in an experiment by Hogg and Turner (1987) involving gender identity. In this study, male and female college students participated in a discussion under one of two conditions. In the personal identity condition, the discussion was between two people of the same sex and the two discussants held different positions on the issue under consideration. In the social identity condition, the discussion group consisted of four people – two males and two females – and the sexes differed on the issue. The latter arrangement was intended to make categorization by sex particularly salient in the setting, and to increase the probability that participants would think of themselves in terms of their gender identity. Following the social interaction, participants in the social identity condition characterized themselves as more typical of their sex and attributed more masculine or feminine traits.to themselves than those in the personal identity condition.

The Hogg and Turner experiment demonstrates that stereotypical traits that may not be particularly relevant to personal identity become central to the self-concept when social identity is activated. When a woman's female identity is not salient, she may think of herself in terms of personal traits that are not relevant to the masculinity–femininity distinction (e.g. as organized, neat, and politically conservative). When her identity as a member of the female category is made salient, however, this same woman may think about herself in terms of those characteristics that make her more like other women and distinct from most men (e.g. nurturant and dependent).

Consistent with this perspective, other experimental research has demonstrated that activation of the "private" self representation increases retrieval of self-cognitions that are quite different from self-cognitions retrieved when the "collective" self-aspect is activated (Trafimow et al. 1991). These results led Trafimow, Triandis and their colleagues to speculate that private and collective self-concepts are stored in separate locations in memory.

Behavioral consequences of group identity

The parallels between egocentrism/personal identity on the one side and ethnocentrism/social identity on the other support the idea that identification with a social group entails a transformation of the sense of self from the individual to the group as a whole (Brewer 1991). When group identification is engaged, goals and motivational biases that function to preserve and enhance the self/ego

(Greenwald 1980) are applied to the ingroup. The implication here is that the transformation goes beyond cognitive representations and self-descriptions. A shift in level of self-definition also has profound effects on motives, intentions, and behavior. In its more dramatic manifestations, the activation of social identities may lead individuals to behave in ways that are contrary to personal self-interest, even at the cost of personal survival.

The potential conflict between individual and collective self-interest is most vividly demonstrated by acts of self-sacrifice associated with warfare or heroic altruism. Individuals dying on behalf of group goals represent an extreme in the difference between behavior directed toward preservation and enhancement of the personal self and behavior motivated by group identification. Less dramatic but none the less significant evidence of disparities between personal and social identity has been obtained in a number of experimental studies. Some of these differences are reviewed below.

Speech style

Although individuals differ in their facility with different languages, dialects, and accents, we are all capable of altering aspects of our style of speech to suit various social occasions (Hymes 1967). Choice of words, certain affectations, use of colloquial expressions, grammatical constructions, etc. can vary depending on how we choose to present ourselves to others. In most social situations, the language we use reflects the aspect of identity that is most salient in that setting (Giles 1978; Giles *et al.* 1980; Giles and Johnson 1981; Sachdev and Bourhis 1990). For bilingual individuals, in particular, language and social identity are closely related (Giles and Byrne 1982).

Experimental research on evaluative ratings of individuals with different dialects or speech styles indicates that hearing "ingroup" speech elicits positive affect toward the speaker (Edwards 1985; Ryan *et al.* 1984). When a region or nation is divided into two or more ethnolinguistic communities, it is often the case that choice of language signals identification with groups that differ in power or status. In general, the language or linguistic style associated with the dominant group is more prestigious, and speech patterns of the subordinate group are derogated or devalued. Under these conditions, members of subordinate ethnic or linguistic groups often exhibit "speech accommodation" (Giles and Smith 1979) in interactions with members of the dominant group, modifying their language style to converge with that of the other speaker.

In contrast to the dynamics of speech accommodation, *ethnolinguistic identity theory* (Giles and Johnson 1981) focuses on the use of divergent speech patterns on the part of subordinate group members, as a method of asserting or expressing distinctive group identity. Bourhis and Giles, for instance, found that adults in Wales accentuated their Welsh accent after hearing a speaker of standard, nonregional English (Giles *et al.* 1977). Similar results were obtained among Flemish speakers in Belgium (Bourhis *et al.* 1979). These findings are particularly interesting when one takes into account the fact that members of low status groups gain advantages *as individuals* when they exhibit accommodation in their speech patterns (Bourhis *et al.* 1975; Giles and Smith 1979). None the less, when group identity is at stake, divergent speech is exhibited despite the social costs incurred.

Polarization of beliefs and attitudes

Self-cognitions include more than abilities and personality traits that we attribute to ourselves. They also include the beliefs and attitudes that we hold as expressions of our values and theories about the world. Decades of research on social influence, conformity, and group decision making has documented the importance of social group membership in shaping attitudes and beliefs (Turner 1991). Of most relevance here is evidence of the effect that social categorization alone can have on the salience, extremity, and commitment with which individuals hold positions on specific social or political issues.

An extremely important outcome of group behavior is the phenomenon of *group polarization*. Positions on issues adopted following a period of group discussion and consensus formation tend to be significantly more extreme than the average positions advocated when individuals express their personal opinions prior to group discussion (Myers and Lamm 1976; Isenberg 1986). This polarization of attitudes associated with group formation has been demonstrated across a wide range of attitude issues and decision tasks.

Most analyses of the group polarization phenomenon focus on the informational and normative social influence that takes place during group discussion. However, some experimental research indicates that the effect of discussion on extremitization of an individual's own attitude is mediated by social identification processes. When the arguments generated in group discussion are tape-recorded and then played to individual subjects (who are alone while they listen to the tape), changes in their attitudes depend on whether the individuals on the tape are identified as members of the listener's ingroup or not. When discussants are not categorized as ingroup members, attitude change, if any, is in the direction of moderate positions expressed in the discussion. However, when the tape is believed to be a discussion among ingroup category members, subjects shift their own attitudes in the direction of the more extreme positions represented on the tape (Mackie and Cooper 1984; Mackie 1986; Wetherell 1987). Further, the listeners perceive the content of the discussion to be more polarized when they think the discussants are ingroup category members than when they do not (Mackie 1986).

These results are consistent with a social identity interpretation of group polarization, which holds that shared identification with a group is a precondition for group polarization (Turner et al. 1989). Ingroup formation is associated with differentiation between ingroup and outgroup categories. On attributes where ingroup and outgroup differ, the ingroup is represented in terms of relatively extreme positions in order to enhance the contrast between groups. Group members then accommodate to the perceived ingroup position as an expression of their social identity. Hence, attitudes associated with salient social identities may be more polarized than personal attitudes, even in the absence of communication or direct social influence. Even when members of the ingroup are not present, focusing attention on group performance or group values can lead to extremitization of individual attitudes (Mackie 1986: Experiment 2; Ng and Wilson 1989).

Bases of attraction

In the research literature on interpersonal attraction, liking between two individuals is strongly related to the similarity between them (Byrne 1971; Byrne et al. 1986). People are likely to become friends or lovers to the extent that they perceive that they are

Figure 2.1   Social categorization theory of group polarization

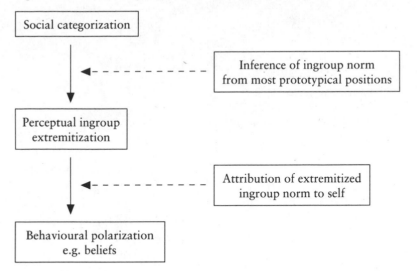

Source: Ng (1989: 7). Reproduced by permission of New Zealand Psychological Society, Inc., copyright holder, *New Zealand Journal of Psychology*.

similar to each other in preferences, attitudes, and values. At this interpersonal level, attraction seems to be a function of the two individuals' personal traits and the degree of match between their individual identities.

On the other hand, research on social categorization and ingroup preference suggests that positive evaluations and liking for other individuals can be induced simply by the knowledge that they share a common group identity. Ingroup members tend to be liked more than outgroup members even when we know nothing about their personal characteristics. In general, we tend to assume that fellow ingroup members are similar to each other, but in this case liking and similarity seem to be a consequence of group formation rather than its cause (Hogg and Turner 1985). As a consequence, ingroup favoritism can occur in the absence of interpersonal attraction or its antecedents.

To represent the idea that liking is sometimes based on group membership alone, Hogg (1992, 1993; Hogg and Hardie 1991) draws a distinction between idiosyncratic personal attraction and depersonalized social attraction. Personal attraction is based on the personal identities of the individuals involved; similarity of personal

Figure 2.2   A model of personal and social attraction

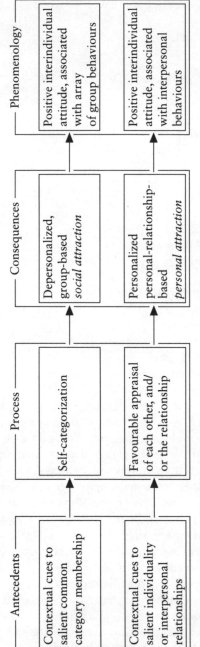

Source: Hogg (1992: 101). Reproduced by permission of the author and Prentice Hall International, Ltd.

interests, attitudes, and values is the primary basis for this form of liking. Social attraction, on the other hand, is based on preferential liking for ingroup over outgroup members. To the extent that a particular group member exemplifies the characteristics that are distinctive or important to that group, that individual will be socially attractive to other ingroup members, regardless of interpersonal similarity.

Figure 2.2 depicts the distinction drawn by Hogg between personal and social attraction. Because these two forms of attraction have different origins, it is possible to display preference for an ingroup member we don't like very much, and to discriminate against a member of an outgroup even if we like that individual personally. Because of this distinction in sources of attraction, it is possible for groups to work together as cohesive units even when members do not like each other interpersonally, a phenomenon that has been demonstrated in laboratory groups (Hogg and Turner 1985) and in real-life groups such as sports teams (e.g. Lenk 1969).

Research by Prentice and colleagues (1994) has also verified the distinction between group identification that is based on direct attachments to the social category, and identification based on interpersonal attachments among group members. In studies of various campus groups, they found that members of groups based on common identity (such as the staff of the school newspaper) were more attached to the group than to fellow group members, whereas members of groups based on interpersonal bonds (such as members of social clubs) were more attached to members of the group overall, and showed a stronger relationship between identification with the group and evaluation of individual group members.

Deprivation and social justice

The distinction between interpersonal relations and intergroup relations is also reflected in the judgments that people make about whether they are being treated fairly or justly. The "relative deprivation" theory of justice (Davis 1959; Runciman 1966) holds that individuals' perceptions of the fairness of their lot in life derives not from the actual value of their outcomes but from comparisons between what they have and what they expected to have. If I have a lot but expected much more, I will feel unjustly treated. If I have very little but expected little, my outcomes will seem fair.

Expected outcomes are determined in part by social comparisons between myself and others. If others have more than I do, I feel deprived. If everyone else is equally deprived, I don't feel so bad. Hence, the experience of deprivation is relative.

People also experience relative deprivation on behalf of their social groups when comparisons are made between their own and other groups. Relative deprivation theorists draw a distinction between perceived deprivation at the personal level and *fraternal deprivation* (Runciman 1966; Vanneman and Pettigrew 1972). Fraternal deprivation arises from comparisons between the outcomes of one's ingroup as a whole and those of other groups, particularly more advantaged outgroups. Fraternal deprivation is more closely associated with ethnic identification than perceptions of personal deprivation (Petta and Walker 1992).

What makes the fraternal deprivation concept particularly interesting is the pervasive finding of a consistent discrepancy between perceptions of discrimination among members of disadvantaged social categories at the individual versus the group levels of comparison. Members of disadvantaged groups report high levels of discrimination against their ingroup. However, the same individuals report much lower levels of discrimination when asked to indicate whether they personally have been discriminated against on the basis of their category membership (Crosby 1982; Taylor *et al.* 1990). There is a significant discontinuity between perceived discrimination at the personal and social levels of identification. But it is discrimination against one's group that is more closely associated with perceived social injustice and desire for social change (Guimond and Dubé-Simard 1983; Walker and Pettigrew 1984).

Cooperation and competition

Group membership also plays an important role in how individuals respond to others when they are in a situation of mutual interdependence. In socially interdependent situations, each person's outcomes are affected by how the others behave. In Chapter 1 we discussed the different kinds of social motives that individuals might bring to such situations. Most important is whether the individual has a cooperative orientation (where the goal is to satisfy the needs and motives of everyone in the group), or a competitive orientation (where the individual is attempting to maximize his or her own outcomes relative to the others).

The distinction between cooperative and competitive intentions is particularly critical in what are called *mixed-motive* situations (Rapoport and Chammah 1965) – relationships in which cooperation between two or more individuals is necessary in order to maximize mutual interests, but where there is also temptation for participants to act competitively in order to serve their individual self-interests. In these situations, if one individual cooperates while the other competes, the competitor comes out ahead and the cooperator loses. However, if both individuals compete, both are worse off than they would be if both cooperated. Thus, competition is a losing strategy in the long run, but cooperation requires trust and concern for the common welfare.

The classic example of a mixed-motive situation is the so-called "prisoner's dilemma," in which each of two individuals must decide whether to cooperate or compete without knowing what the other will do. The name comes from an anecdote in which two suspected criminals are arrested and placed in separate rooms where they are isolated from each other. Then each is given the following choice: if you confess and the other guy does not, then you will go free and he will be sent to prison for 20 years; if you do not confess but he does, then you will be the one sent to prison and he will go free. If you both confess, both of you will get ten years in prison. However, if neither of you confesses, you will both get only five years on a reduced charge. Clearly, in this dilemma, the two criminals are best off if they do not confess. But each individual must make this decision without knowing what the other is doing – if one holds out and does not confess while the other one makes a confession, the hold-out will be severely penalized. If there is any element of distrust between the two criminals, both will confess. (This is obviously what the sheriff in this story has in mind!)

Social psychologists have turned this choice dilemma into a "game" situation in which players are faced with the decision represented in Figure 2.3. Here, the outcomes represent gains or losses of money or other valued commodities, rather than the prison terms from the original dilemma. In the laboratory version, players are given a choice between two responses – one labeled "C" and the other labeled "D". Choosing C provides the best possible outcomes for both players combined, but choosing D gives each player a chance to win while the other loses. However, if both choose D, both come out worse than if they had chosen C.

Figure 2.3   The "prisoner's dilemma" game

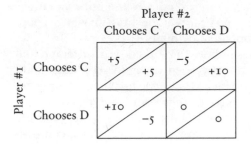

(Value to the left of each diagonal represents the outcome to player #1, value to the right is outcome to player #2)

Years of experimental research with the prisoner's dilemma paradigm has helped to identify under what conditions pairs of individuals will develop mutual cooperation in response to the dilemma, and when they will "lock in" to competitive responding in which both lose in the long run (Oskamp and Perlman 1965; Rapoport and Chammah 1965). One factor that seems to influence choices in the dilemma situation is category membership of the two participants. Even though the players are strangers to each other, if they know that they share some common ingroup membership they are more likely to enter into cooperative responding than if they do not have a shared category membership (Wilson and Kayatani 1968; Dion 1973; Prentice and Miller 1992).

The effect of ingroup membership on cooperative behavior has been observed beyond the two-person situation. When the prisoner's dilemma is generalized to groups of more than two people, it is known as a *social dilemma* (Messick and Brewer 1983). Social dilemmas are choice situations in which individuals acting in their own self-interest make decisions that lead to collective disaster. Many real-world problems such as conservation of scarce resources, environmental pollution, waste disposal, and depletion of the ozone layer are examples of large-scale social dilemmas. In social dilemmas individuals are, in effect, faced with a conflict between their own individual self-interest and collective welfare. In laboratory experiments involving social dilemma choices, group identity has been found to make a significant difference in individual behavior. When a collection of individuals believe that they share a common ingroup membership they are more likely to act in the interest of collective welfare than individuals in the same situation who do not have a sense of group identity (Kramer and Brewer 1984; Brewer and Kramer 1986).

Identification with ingroups, then, can elicit cooperative behavior even in the absence of interpersonal communication among group members. Within the ingroup category, individuals develop a co-operative orientation toward shared problems. What happens, how-ever, when dilemmas involve two or more groups of individuals? In an important program of research, Insko and his colleagues have demonstrated a significant discontinuity between individual and group behavior in social dilemma situations. When two unrelated individuals make decisions in a prisoner's dilemma setting they are much more likely to make cooperative choices than when deci-sions are made by individuals who represent two different social categories (McCallum et al. 1985; Insko et al. 1987, 1990).

As can be seen in Table 2.1, decisions made by groups are con-sistently and significantly more competitive than decisions made by lone individuals in the same setting. The same competitive orienta-tion is obtained when individuals make decisions on behalf of, or as representatives of, a social group (Insko et al. 1987). A similar effect has been found in laboratory experiments on social dilemmas. When a collective is divided into distinct subcategories, individuals behave less cooperatively (and are more likely to destroy the collect-ive welfare) than when the group is undifferentiated (Kramer and Brewer 1984).

The clear implication of this research is that social identity has very different effects on cooperation depending on whether the interdependence is within or between social groups. When social identity is salient, individuals adopt a cooperative orientation toward fellow ingroup members and are likely to behave in ways that promote group welfare rather than individual self-interest. On the other hand, they are also more likely to adopt a competitive orientation toward individuals who are members of outgroups, even when they face a common problem (Brewer and Schneider 1990). When individuals interact in terms of their social identities, it makes a big difference whether the situation is an intragroup or an intergroup exchange.

Overview

The evidence from a number of different domains of social behavior supports a distinction between behavior motivated by identification

Table 2.1 Prisoner's Dilemma Game: cooperation by individuals versus groups

		Mean no. cooperative plays	Mean joint cooperation	Mean joint competition
McCallum et al. (1985) Experiment 1	Individuals	13.70	5.57	1.87
	Pairs	7.57	2.07	4.37
McCallum et al. (1985) Experiment 2	Individuals	14.94	6.25	1.12
	Pairs	9.25	3.37	4.00
Insko et al. (1987)	Individuals	18.68	9.45	0.21
	3-person groups	12.77	5.41	3.18
Insko et al. (1990) Study 2	Individuals	19.00	–	–
	3-person groups	9.86	–	–

with social groups and behavior motivated by personal self-interest. When a particular group identity is engaged, individuals act in ways that represent and maintain distinctive group characteristics, even when that behavior is not consistent with individual egocentric motives. On the one side, social identity enhances liking, trust, and cooperation toward fellow ingroup members, as well as actions that promote collective welfare. On the other hand, social identity also engages preferential biases, extreme attitudes, and competitive orientation toward members of outgroups – all conditions that promote the likelihood of intergroup conflict.

Thus motives and behaviors that derive from attachment and loyalty to ingroups have important implications for *inter*group relations. Before we turn to intergroup settings, however, we should give some attention to various theoretical perspectives that have been advanced to explain why we become attached to ingroups in the first place.

Theories of group identification

Human sociobiology

Theories of human evolution must take into account the overwhelming evidence that the human species evolved in the context of group living (Caporael and Brewer 1991). Much of the speculation about species-specific traits and abilities derives from analysis of the survival requirements associated with living in hunter-gatherer societies (e.g. Buss 1990, 1991). Sociobiological models of the evolution of human social behavior rest heavily on the notion of *inclusive fitness*. These models assume that the gene is the basic unit of selection, and that selection favors genes that produce behavior benefitting anyone who carries those genes, including other individuals who possess the same genes by common descent or kin relationships (Archer 1991).

One implication of this model of evolution is that there is a genetic disposition to behave differentially toward "insiders" (kin and extended family likely to share common genes) and "outsiders" (nonkin, outgroups). This idea is the basis for a "sociobiology of ethnocentrism" (van den Berghe 1981; Reynolds *et al.* 1987), which holds that ethnocentric behavior derives from self-interested pursuit of inclusive genetic fitness. Cooperation between individuals will occur only to the extent that they have a high proportion of shared genes, since helping close relatives perpetuates one's own genes. Conversely, the likelihood of conflict between individuals or groups of individuals increases as the proportion of shared genes decreases (van den Berghe 1981: 7).

According to the sociobiological view, the primal ethnic group is the small band of 100–200 related individuals, within which the human propensity for cooperative social arrangements is presumed to have evolved. Ethnocentric preference is extended to larger social groups through the development of "markers" (skin pigmentation, hair and facial features, mannerisms, etc.) which signal genetic relatedness among unfamiliar individuals (Johnson 1986, 1989). One model goes so far as to postulate an evolved "identification mechanism" that provides for selective attachment to large groups that best promote the interests of the nucleus (kin-based) ethnic group (Shaw and Wong 1989).

Other biological models of ethnocentrism and xenophobia preceded the sociobiological perspective, including ethological theories of territoriality and aggression (e.g. Eibl-Eibesfeldt 1979). Collectively, these theories link ingroup formation to ethnocentric aggression and the inevitability of warfare, both of which are discussed further in later chapters.

Psychodynamic theories

Freudian theory departs somewhat from evolution-based biological models in assigning a greater role to experience and development in the origin of ethnocentric identification. Freud's own theory of group identification centered on the role of the group leader as the object of identification (Freud 1921/1960). Neo-Freudian "object relations theory" (Klein 1975; Ashbach and Schermer 1987) extended the theory to incorporate all symbolic representations of the group as objects of identification. According to this view, social identity is the product of projection of the self on to external objects and introjection/incorporation of objects into the sense of self.

Freud also coined the phrase "narcissism of minor differences" to refer to the apparent preoccupation of group members with small or trivial distinctions that maintain differentiation between groups (Freud 1912/1957). Volkan (1988) used this as a basis for a theory of identity formation that holds that individual identity is achieved through a universal process of defining "allies" and "enemies." The process begins in the first few months of life as the infant bonds with the primary caretaker and learns to distinguish familiar others from strangers. This process of we–they differentiation (along with associated affect) continues as a basis for achieving a stable definition of self.

Unlike sociobiological explanations, psychoanalytic theories of group identification assume that self-relevant groups are defined by experience and culture rather than kinship. None the less, the psychoanalytic version of social identity formation is an intensely individual one in that groups are essentially projections of the *personal* self, a product of individual development and interpersonal experiences.

Social comparison theory

Moving to more truly social psychological perspectives, a classic theory of group formation is provided by Festinger's (1954) social comparison theory of affiliation. Prior to the publication of the formal theory of social comparison, Festinger published an earlier version of the theory which focused on the processes of communication and consensus formation in small groups (Festinger 1950). His purpose in this earlier paper was to explain why members of groups tend to be so similar in attitudes, values, and behavior.

A basic premise of Festinger's explanation was the idea that people need a sense of subjective validity for their beliefs about themselves and the world around them. Much of our knowledge or understanding about the world we live in does not come from direct personal experience. We may come to learn that ice is cold and walls are solid by direct contact with these objects, but much of our knowledge about what is right or true – especially our knowledge about social groups and social behaviors – has no such objective referent. In order to achieve a sense of validation of such beliefs, people engage in "social reality testing." Beliefs are seen as valid or appropriate when they are shared by similar others, i.e. by members of appropriate reference groups. The more uncertain an individual is about the correctness of a belief or attitude, the more important it becomes to find consensual support for that belief. Similarity to reference groups induces stability and confidence in one's own perceptions.

The effect of uncertainty on seeking the company of similar others was first demonstrated experimentally in a classic study by Schachter (1959). In this experiment, female students arrived at the research laboratory and learned that their participation would involve receiving a series of electric shocks. In one experimental condition, the participant was reassured in advance that the shocks would be mild and safe. In the alternative experimental treatment, the description of the upcoming shocks was somewhat more ominous. What Schachter was trying to do with these experimental variations was to induce different levels of fear and uncertainty in the research participants. Those who were given reassurances about the nature of the electric shock were assumed to be in a state of low uncertainty and little fear. Those who had been led to anticipate something more severe were assumed to be in a state of relatively high fear and uncertainty about what would happen to them.

At this point in the experiment the researcher explained to the student that it would take about ten minutes to set up the laboratory equipment and that during that time she could wait in another room. Each participant was given a choice between waiting alone in a separate waiting room, or in a classroom down the hall "with some of the other girls here" who were participating in the same experiment. As expected on the basis of Festinger's social comparison theory, women in the high fear/uncertainty condition showed more desire to be with others than did those in the low fear condition. Out of 32 participants in the high fear condition, 20 expressed a clear preference to wait with others, whereas only ten out of 30 in the low fear condition had such a preference.

Schachter believed that uncertainty led to the need to be with others, but only with others who were similar to themselves, facing the same situation. This was demonstrated in a later version of the experiment in which participants, after being put through the high fear condition, were again given a choice between waiting alone or with others down the hall. But this time, the others were *not* participants in the experiment but students waiting for an exam. With that option, *none* of the research participants chose to wait with others. Apparently affiliation to reduce uncertainty is selective – only the ingroup will do.

Agreeing with members of one's ingroup apparently increases certainty and subjective validity of beliefs and attitudes (Darley 1966). Finding out that others disagree reduces certainty – but only if those others are ingroup members. Learning that outgroupers do not share our opinions or values does not shake our confidence in the correctness of those beliefs (Orive 1988). On many issues of values and preferences we expect to agree with ingroup members but not necessarily with everyone. Thus only ingroup members count as sources of validation, at least for subjective judgments (Gorenflo and Crano 1989).

Social identity and self-categorization theory

Social comparison theory is essentially an interpersonal theory of group formation and attachment. According to such theories, individuals seek similar others to satisfy needs for social reality and self-definition; ingroups are derived from this process of mutual affiliation among individuals. Social identity theory provides an alternative account of group formation and social influence (Turner 1991).

As originally articulated by Tajfel and Turner (Tajfel 1981; Turner 1984; Tajfel and Turner 1986), social identity theory was largely a response to the prevailing interpersonal models of group formation, such as social comparison theory (Hogg 1992). The basic premise of social identity theorists was that ingroup–outgroup distinctions arise from social categorization processes. Accentuation of category differences, combined with a need for positive distinctiveness (inter*group* social comparison), results in ingroup favoritism. The important point is that ingroup classification *precedes* rather than derives from interpersonal processes.

Further elaboration of the cognitive underpinnings of group formation and ingroup preference is represented by Turner's *self-categorization theory* (SCT) (Turner et al. 1987). From this perspective, personal and social identity differ in that they represent different levels of abstraction (inclusiveness) for self-categorization. Which level of categorization predominates in self-perception is a function of the situation or frame of reference at a given time. Within a frame of reference, categorizing follows the principles of *meta-contrast* (Turner 1985; Oakes 1987). A subset of persons are categorized as a single entity to the degree that differences among those within the category are less than differences between them and the others within the comparative context.

There is, of necessity, a functional conflict between different levels of categorization of the same stimulus situation. Since categorization results in accentuations of similarity within categories (assimilation) and of differences between categories (contrast), the salience of one level of categorization produces intraclass similarities and interclass differences that reduce or inhibit perceived similarities and differences at other levels. Thus self-categorization at the intergroup level (social identity) is incompatible with categorization at the interpersonal level. This underlies the SCT explanation for the self-stereotyping effects cited earlier in this chapter. A shift toward social identity entails a depersonalization of individual self-perception, perceiving oneself as a representative of the ingroup category possessing those characteristics that distinguish the ingroup from relevant outgroups. According to SCT, it is this depersonalization of self-perception that underlies basic group phenomena, including ethnocentrism, cooperation, emotional contagion, and conformity to group norms (Turner 1985; Turner et al. 1987).

Motivational theories of social identification

As a version of social identity theory, SCT is heavily cognitive, emphasizing the categorization processes underlying group identification to the exclusion of most motivational and affective processes (Hogg and Abrams 1993). Other variations of social identity theory accept the basic premiss of categorization but add various motivational components to account for the emotional and behavioral consequences of ingroup identification.

Common fate

Jacob Rabbie has criticized social identity theory (and SCT more specifically) for failing to recognize perceived interdependence among individual members of a collective as the defining characteristic of a social group (Rabbie and Horwitz 1988; Rabbie et al. 1989). Perceived interdependence derives from experiencing *common fate*, which Rabbie regards as a precondition for the emergence of group norms, group identification, and shared social identities. In this view, social identity derives ultimately from self-interest, under conditions in which each individual's outcomes are linked to the outcomes of others. Positive interdependence produces cooperation and ingroup formation. Negative interdependence produces conflict and differentiation.

It is not always clear from the experimental procedures that Rabbie uses to induce "common fate" whether shared outcomes necessarily involve true interdependence. Interdependence means that one person's outcomes are affected directly by the behavior of another individual in achieving his or her own outcomes. In a highly interdependent situation such as a team sport, each individual's opportunities and successes are determined in part by the actions of other team members, and the coordination among their actions. However, individuals can share the same outcomes without interdependence in that sense. For example, three people standing at the same bus stop in the rain are experiencing the same fate (getting cold and wet) without their outcomes being in any way determined by the behavior (or outcomes) of the other group members. If one member of the group chooses to get in out of the rain, this does not affect how wet the others get. Similarly, members of a specific social category may receive the same treatment from some external body without creating interpersonal interdependence among category members. Yet if this kind of common fate can produce ingroup identification – as the results of Rabbie's own experiments suggest it can (Rabbie and Horwitz 1969) – then interdependence is not a necessary condition for group formation. Perceived interdependence may be a product of common fate, rather than its source.

With or without actual interdependence, perceptions of shared interests or common fate do seem to be crucial to the emergence of collective identity. Gurin and Townsend (1986) found that a sense of common fate (perceived common treatment and outcomes as a function of category membership) proved to be the most important predictor of collective orientation in a study of gender consciousness and political activism. And Prentice and Miller (1992) argue that identification can be based on bonding produced by distinctive shared experiences, such as having the same birthday.

Self-esteem
Even more controversial than the issue of interdependence is that of the role of social identity in maintenance of positive self-esteem (Abrams and Hogg 1988; Crocker *et al.* 1993). There seems little doubt that individuals do derive benefit from their group's successes and achievements, even when that individual has not contributed directly to the group's accomplishment (Cialdini *et al.* 1976). One experiment found that after sports fans watched a live

basketball game, their estimates of their own personal skills were influenced by the outcome of the game. When their team was successful, fans predicted that they would perform better in a later experimental task than when their own team had lost (Hirt et al. 1992). This is consistent with social identity theory's contention that an individual's sense of self-worth is enhanced by positive distinctiveness of his or her ingroup. In general, individuals have been found to identify more strongly with experimentally created groups that are successful and have high status (Ellemers et al. 1988).

Findings such as these have led some theorists to conclude that group identification is motivated by the need for self-enhancement. In other words, individuals seek to identify with high status groups in order to repair or maintain positive self-esteem. However, there is little direct evidence that the need for self-enhancement underlies ingroup identification. For one thing, individuals with low self-esteem do not value ingroups more positively than individuals whose self-esteem is already high – if anything, it is the other way around, with high self-esteem individuals showing greater ingroup identification (Crocker and Schwartz 1985; Crocker et al. 1987).

The self-esteem explanation is further undermined by evidence of strong identification with disadvantaged or low status ingroups. Some experimental research indicates that social identification with a group may actually be increased when the group is threatened or stigmatized. Results of an experiment by Turner and his colleagues (Turner et al. 1984) demonstrated that when individuals are committed to group membership, ingroup defeat produced even higher levels of ingroup preference than did success (see Figure 2.4).

These results from laboratory experiments parallel findings from field studies of members of disadvantaged or stigmatized groups. Many studies now indicate that identification with such groups is associated with high rather than low individual self-esteem (Rosenberg 1979; Cross 1985; Crocker and Major 1989). Overall, research in this area supports the idea that positive ingroup evaluation and collective self-esteem is the product of group identification rather than its cause.

Self-verification

Apart from enhancement of positive self-esteem, recent theories of self-development postulate a number of other motivational factors that influence the construction of an individual's self-concept.

Figure 2.4   Ingroup attachment following success or failure

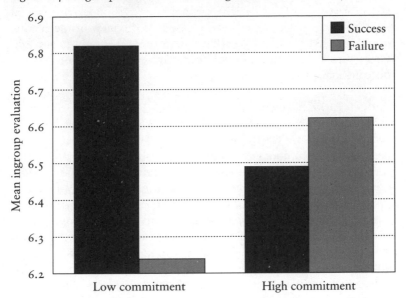

Source: Turner *et al.* (1984). Experiment 1

Foremost among these is the need for *self-verification* (Swann 1987) – the drive to establish and maintain a consistent, coherent self-image. Abrams and Hogg (1988; Hogg and Abrams 1993) propose that it is this need for self-definition that is the primary motivational basis for social identification.

Like Festinger's social comparison theory, this version of social identity theory assumes that group formation ultimately derives from the need to reduce uncertainty. However, instead of inter-personal social comparison as the basis for self-definition, this theory focuses on the role of group consensus as the basis for coherence and subjective certainty. As Hogg and Abrams (1993: 189) put it, "uncertainty-reduction is an individual motivation, but one that inevitably can only be realized by group belongingness." This accounts for the strong tendency to polarize representations of the ingroup on dimensions that distinguish it from other groups, and for group members' willingness to conform to group norms and stereotypes in the interests of maintaining intergroup distinctions.

Hogg and Abrams (1993) go so far as to suggest that enhanced self-esteem is a consequence of the uncertainty reduction achieved through group consensus and social identity. From this perspective, subjective certainty is the primary motive underlying social identification; positive self-esteem is a secondary or derivative motivation. At the level of social identity, self-enhancement and self-verification are not competing motives but aspects of a single motivational process.

Optimal distinctiveness

For group membership to satisfy an individual's need for meaning and coherence, the clarity of the boundary that separates ingroup membership from nonmembership becomes particularly important. Therefore theories based on self-verification call attention to the importance of the distinctiveness of social categories as a factor in group identification. Distinctiveness incorporates both category salience and the exclusiveness of group membership as properties of specific social categories. In a recent variation of self-categorization theory, Brewer (1991) has provided a model of the psychological motives underlying the preference for distinctive social identities.

Brewer's *optimal distinctiveness theory* postulates that human beings have two powerful social motives: a need for *inclusion* which is satisfied by assimilation of the self into larger collectives, and an opposing need for *differentiation* which is satisfied by distinguishing the self from others. Groups that are exclusive rather than highly inclusive engage more attachment and identification because they satisfy both of these needs simultaneously. Distinctive social identities meet the individual's need for inclusion (intracategory assimilation) while at the same time serving the need for differentiation between self and others (intercategory contrast). According to this model, distinctive *social* identities should be more satisfying than *personal* identity as the preferred level of self-categorization.

Optimal distinctiveness theory accounts for the pervasive finding that social identification and ingroup favoritism is greater for members of minority groups than among majority group members (Mullen *et al.* 1992a). This group size effect has been obtained in both laboratory and field studies, although effects in the real world are complicated by the frequent confounding of minority status with other social disadvantages. However, experimental evidence indicates that when the need for differentiation is activated, individuals value minority category membership more than membership in majority groups, regardless of other status differentials between ingroup and outgroup (Brewer *et al.* 1993).

Status versus distinction

Because minority size is often associated with disadvantages in status or power, in many contexts group distinctiveness and positive evaluation may be negatively related. Members of low status minorities may face a conflict between group identification based on optimal distinctiveness and preference for positive social identity. Similarly, for members of stigmatized groups, self-verification of social identity may conflict with the need for self-enhancement. In the study by Hogg and Turner (1987) cited earlier, for instance, when categorization by sex was made highly salient both male and female subjects accentuated the sex-typicality of their own self-perceptions. However, for females this self-categorization resulted in lowered self-esteem, compared to conditions in which sex categorization was not so salient.

To protect self-esteem, individuals may actively distance themselves from their group identity, at least with respect to those attributes that are contained in the negative group stereotype (Gibbons 1985; Gibbons et al. 1991). On the other hand, negative attributes may have less impact on individual self-esteem if they are perceived as group characteristics rather than distinctive personal traits (Coates and Winston 1983; Crocker and Major 1989). In that case, self-esteem may actually be enhanced by self-stereotyping as a typical group member since it alters the context in which negative traits or experiences are evaluated. Minority group members can embrace their distinctive group identity, but sometimes at the cost of rejecting or defying majority criteria for positive evaluation (Steele 1992).

The conditions under which members of disadvantaged minorities will adopt a strong group identity and commit themselves to collective action on behalf of group interests have long been of concern to social and political psychologists (e.g. Gurin et al. 1980; Tajfel and Turner 1986; Wright et al. 1990). We will consider further research and theory on this issue in later chapters.

Do ingroups require outgroups?

Discussion of the importance of meaningful intergroup differentiation as a determinant of social identification raises the issue of the social context within which ingroups are defined. Defining what the ingroup *is* also requires defining what it is *not* (Allen et al. 1983). As Tajfel and Forgas (1981: 124) put it, "we are what we are because *they* are not what we are . . ." But who constitutes this ambiguous "they?" Are relevant others limited to members of specific contrasting groups, or could "they" refer to all other human beings who are excluded from membership in the ingroup?

Both theory and research are ambiguous on this issue of the need for specific outgroups as a factor in ingroup identity. Almost all initial experimental research on social identity was undertaken in the context of specific ingroup–outgroup comparisons, and the notion of "positive distinctiveness" is usually understood to mean comparisons between the status of the ingroup and specific, relevant outgroups. Ingroup attraction and perceived similarity have both been found to be enhanced when ingroup members are evaluated in the context of salient outgroups (Wagner and Ward 1993). Further, there is evidence that the presence of symbols of an outgroup is sufficient to arouse awareness of *ingroup* identity (Wilder and Shapiro 1984), demonstrating the reciprocal relationship between ingroup and outgroup salience.

But although specific intergroup comparisons may enhance ingroup awareness, this does not mean that such contrasts are a necessary condition for social identification. More recent experimental work being undertaken with respect to self-categorization theory is exploring the effects of group formation *per se*, in the absence of any explicit intergroup context (Turner *et al.* 1987; Hogg 1992). In an earlier review of ingroup bias research, Brewer (1979) suggested that the existence of an identifiable outgroup may not be essential to ingroup favoritism. Differentiated social groupings may be only one mechanism by which the self is included in a bounded social unit. The perception of common fate and shared distinctiveness may be achievable without reference to specific outgroups, although the presence of outgroups may influence the nature or intensity of affect or emotions attached to ingroup membership.

If ingroup identification does not depend on explicit outgroups, then the consequences of ingroup favoritism and attachment may be manifest in the absence of hostility toward or derogation of outgroup members. Preferential treatment of those who share a common category membership produces biases that benefit the ingroup over noningroup members even without any negative prejudices against outgroups. By the same token, some forms of discrimination may be motivated by outgroup hatred, in the absence of any specific ingroup loyalties. What may account for such outgroup hostility is the subject of the following chapter.

Further reading

Brewer, M. B. (1991). The social self: On being the same and different at the same time. *Personality and Social Psychology Bulletin*, 17, 475–82. The optimal distinctiveness theory of the motivations underlying group identification.

Crocker, J. and Major, B. (1989). Social stigma and self-esteem: The self-protective properties of stigma. *Psychological Review*, 96, 608–30. A review of the role of group identification in protecting individuals from the negative effects of stigmatization.

Hogg, M. A. (1992). *The social psychology of group cohesiveness: From attraction to social identity*. London: Harvester Wheatsheaf. Ingroup attachment and morale from the perspective of social identity theory.

Hogg, M. A. and Abrams, D. (eds) (1993). *Group motivation: Social psychological perspectives*. London: Harvester Wheatsheaf. An edited volume of papers on the motivations underlying group behavior.

Turner, J. C., Hogg, M., Oakes, P., Reicher, S. and Wetherell, M. (1987). *Rediscovering the social group: A self-categorization theory*. Oxford: Basil Blackwell. A cognitive theory of group identification and self-concept.

3 / PREJUDICE AND OUTGROUP HOSTILITY: WHEN DIFFERENCE IS BAD

> Anyone can become angry – that is easy, but to be angry with the right person, to the right degree, at the right time, for the right purpose, and in the right way – this is not easy.
>
> (Aristotle, *Nicomachean Ethics* II.ix)

Chapter 2 described ingroup bias and the processes that are invoked in forming and maintaining a positive ingroup identity, or a sense of we-ness. The belief that our group, or we, are good – that is, that the attributes, dispositions, and values, of our own social group are superior – strengthens our individual feeling of personal self-worth. In this chapter we examine the inverse – outgroup derogation, the belief that "they" are bad. If, as Tajfel (1979) reasoned, "we are what we are because they are not what we are," what are the psychological processes by which we select and maintain we–they, or ingroup–outgroup distinctions and boundaries? In their efforts to understand them, researchers have looked to cognitive and affective processes, as well as situational forces that influence our perceptions of, and behaviors toward, outgroup members.

In the past three decades, the dominant approach to understanding reactions to outgroup members has focused on cognitive process, with a particular emphasis on how we attend to, interpret, and remember information about outgroups or members of outgroups (see Devine *et al.* 1994). More recently, however, interest has begun to shift toward affective and emotional responses, in an attempt to understand how cognition is affected by other internal states such as negative and positive mood, and levels of anxiety or arousal (see Sorrentino and Higgins 1986; Sorrentino and Short 1986). As elegantly stated by Hamilton and Mackie (1993: 4–5):

contemporary thinking about cognition and affect emphasizes a more integrative relationship between these two systems. Cognition has its impact on affect by constituting the appraisal processes that regulate the social and cultural interpretation of experienced emotion. At the same time, affect has its effects on judgments and behavior through its impact on cognitive processes. Affect activates motivations or goal states, which in turn influence the extent and nature of further processing. In addition, arousal level and affective states influence what information is attended to and what contents will be activated from memory, thereby exerting control over the raw material that becomes the grist for the information processing mill. Thus, affect and cognition are mutually interactive components of a broader system.

Though the psychological processes we will discuss are mutually influential and have aspects that overlap, it will be helpful first to consider each separately. We begin with recent research on cognition of outgroups. Next we discuss the biasing influences of emotion or affect on perception. Last, we consider situational factors that affect aggression – the expression or inhibition of outgroup derogation or hostility. Figure 3.1 presents a model showing the interplay of these factors. Note that cognition and affect mutually influence one another, as well as having effects on attitudes and behavior toward the outgroup. Note too that situational factors are shown as moderating the effects of cognitions and affect on attitudes and behavior toward the outgroup.

Outgroup homogeneity and the accentuation of group differences

One widely studied aspect of outgroup perception is the tendency to see outgroup members as "all alike" – especially in circumstances where group memberships are salient (Mullen and Hu 1989). This "homogenization" of the outgroup is particularly strong with respect to attributes that do in fact characterize the outgroup (Lee and Ottati 1993) and for trait dimensions that most distinguish the outgroup from the ingroup (Stangor and Ford 1992).

One source of evidence about outgroup homogeneity comes from the narrative descriptions people provide when they are talking

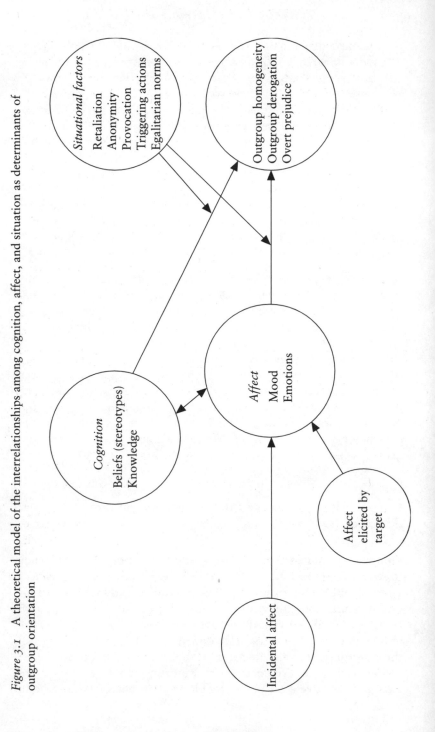

Figure 3.1 A theoretical model of the interrelationships among cognition, affect, and situation as determinants of outgroup orientation

about ingroups or outgroups. When describing outgroups, we are less likely to mention different subtypes within the larger outgroup category (Park *et al.* 1992). For example, business students as well as engineering students might both describe engineering students as generally hard working and studious. But, when viewing engineering students, business majors would not readily differentiate among subgroups of engineering students that engineering students themselves see as distinct. Engineering students might note, for instance, that some engineering students study hard because they really enjoy the courses, some study hard primarily to meet their parents' expectations, and others study hard mainly in order to improve their chances of getting a good job when they graduate. Business students, on the other hand, would not distinguish amongst the three subtypes of outgroup members, all of whom exhibit the stereotypic trait ascribed to engineers, namely, hard working.

The belief that outgroup members are highly similar, or essentially interchangeable, means that one can use group-based stereotypes to judge and interpret an individual outgroup person's behavior. If outgroups are seen as homogeneous, there is little motivation to attend to individual individuating information about an outgroup member, or to acquire new information which might serve to correct stereotyped views of that person. Thus the tendency to perceive outgroups as homogeneous and undifferentiated is one important factor in understanding the perpetuation of stereotypes about social categories.

Explanations of outgroup homogeneity

Theory and research suggests numerous explanations of outgroup homogeneity. Some of these explanations are primarily cognitive, emphasizing the types of information that are likely to be attended to, stored, and accessed when relevant. Other explanations emphasize instead motives or goals that can be fulfilled or achieved as a consequence of holding a homogeneous view of the outgroup.

Cognitive explanations
One cognitive explanation of outgroup homogeneity rests on the salience and the richness of self-perception. We know our own complexities and inconsistencies. We know the full array of our interests, desires, achievements and failures, our attitudes, beliefs,

and values. Thus the self is seen as highly differentiated (Markus and Wurth 1987). Because people typically view themselves as unique and differentiated, they might project this same view on to others, as the result of the pervasive tendency of assuming similarity between themselves and others (Mullen *et al.* 1985; Marks and Miller 1987; Dawes 1989; Spears and Manstead 1990). However, the self is also seen as a member of the ingroup. People think about the self more frequently when making ingroup judgments than when making outgroup judgments (Park and Judd 1990). They also assume more similarity between themselves and the ingroup than between themselves and the outgroup (Holtz and Miller 1985; Miller *et al.* 1991; Mullen *et al.* 1992b). When considered together, these ingredients imply a relative homogeneity effect in one's perceptions of the outgroup, compared to perceptions of an ingroup.

Another theoretical account of outgroup homogeneity is that of Linville and her colleagues (e.g. Linville and Jones 1980; Linville 1982; Linville *et al.* 1986; Linville *et al.* 1989). In this model, differences in familiarity are postulated to explain the degree to which one or another group is seen as more or less variable. Because we spend considerably more time with ingroup members than with outgroup members, we are more familiar with them, we notice more instances of differences among them, differences in the types of persons that they are. By contrast, members of an outgroup are typically unfamiliar. Because they belong to an outgroup category, one does not have as much contact with them. And when one does have contact, it is likely to be of a much less intimate nature than that which characterizes most contact with ingroup members. This difference in the richness and complexity of information that has been collected and stored with respect to ingroup and outgroup members consequently accounts for why the outgroup is seen as more homogeneous.

Apart from the frequency of interactions with ingroup and outgroup members, recent research suggests that information obtained from interaction with ingroup and outgroup members is stored in quite different ways. When people interact with ingroup members, they store information in connection with the individual person, such as the person's name. By contrast, information about outgroup members is stored in terms of general attribute categories (Ostrom *et al.* 1993). Thus, when Sam recalls information about other men he just met at his friend's bachelor party, he might tend to recall that Jack's favorite TV show is *Wide World of Sports*, and his favorite sport is boxing, or that Harry appears to be highly anxious, is an Art major, and likes to collect compact discs. When, instead, he attempts to recall information about the women (an outgroup) he met at his wife's afternoon tea, the richness and accuracy of recall about specific traits associated with the names of the women at the party will be noticeably inferior. More interesting is that information about the outgroup is better recalled in terms of attribute categories – what kinds of TV shows the women liked, what organizations they had joined, and so on. That is, information about the ingroup is organized around the names of actors. By contrast, information about the outgroup is organized instead around the attribute dimensions which characterize members of that social category: the types of jobs women hold, the types of TV shows they prefer, or the types of sports they like. The information about the attributes of a social category contributes to stereotyped views of that category, rather than creating individuated views about its individual members, and thereby augments perceptions of homogeneity among outgroup categories.

Motivational explanations
Although the outgroup homogeneity effect can be accounted for with cognitive explanations, a number of more motivational explanations may also account for the effect. One possible source of motivation is the need for a positive social identity. Our Western notion of personhood is strongly linked to an individuated perception. The proposition that individual complexity (or heterogeneity) is a positive trait is readily illustrated by thinking of the associations you have to the word "simpleton." Although, as previously indicated, people reliably tend to see themselves as more similar to others (or others as more similar to self) than reality warrants (Mullen *et al.* 1985; Marks and Miller 1987), this pervasive tendency is countered by an opposing motivation to be unique or distinctive from others (Snyder and Fromkin 1980; Marks 1984; Goethals *et al.* 1991). From this latter perspective, perceiving the outgroup as homogeneous implicitly augments one's self-perception of uniqueness.

The anxiety often associated with being among outgroup persons (Stephan and Stephan 1985) provides another source of motivation for perceptions of outgroup homogeneity. We tend to feel uncomfortable in strange settings. We feel apprehensive when we are unsure about what will happen next. Strangeness or unfamiliarity is often a precursor of anxiety. Because we are less familiar with outgroup persons, imagining or being with them is likely to trigger anxious thoughts (Wilder and Shapiro 1989a). The perception of homogeneity increases predictability or controllability. Thus, exaggerating the degree to which outgroup members share attributes in common should augment the perception that their behavior is predictable.

Ambivalence/amplification theory is a more complex motivational explanation that applies particularly to the relation between a dominant, politically powerful group (such as whites in the US) and a less powerful or disadvantaged minority group (such as blacks). It emphasizes the conflict between egalitarian values and antipathy toward the outgroup. On the one hand whites hold pro-black feelings that stem from the endorsement of egalitarianism and fairness as laudable values, and they simultaneously perceive that blacks are disadvantaged. Concomitantly, these same whites possess anti-black feelings that arise from perceptions that blacks deviate from traditional cultural values, such as the Protestant work ethic. In turn, these ambivalent feelings motivate exaggerated evaluations of blacks. Thus the model predicts that in comparison with how whites respond to other whites, their conflicted feelings about black Americans lead them to evaluate them more extremely – either more extremely positive or more extremely negative, depending on the situation. And the more strongly a white American simultaneously holds these conflicting motives toward blacks, the more extreme these evaluations will be.

According to the ambivalence/amplification model, when a black individual and a white individual exhibit the same positive behavior, the black will be evaluated more positively than the white; conversely, a black behaving negatively will be evaluated more harshly than a white who behaves in that same manner. And to the degree that evaluative responses are displaced toward the endpoints of the scale, there will be a more restricted range and more outgroup homogeneity associated with evaluations of black as opposed to white targets.

Accentuation of group differences

In addition to the ingroup favoritism discussed in Chapter 2 and perceptions of outgroup homogeneity discussed above, a third persistent phenomenon in intergroup perceptions is the overestimation of between-group differences. Group members exaggerate the degree to which the outgroup differs from the ingroup. This maximization of difference has been termed the *accentuation effect*. Although exaggeration of the differences between categories can be demonstrated in the absence of ingroup–outgroup distinctions (Campbell 1956; Tajfel and Wilkes 1963), and can occur solely as a function of cognitive processes (Krueger 1992), the motivational explanations that we previously discussed in relation to outgroup homogeneity seem directly relevant to the accentuation effects found in the relations between real groups. Exaggeration of outgroup differentness is particularly likely on moral dimensions and judgments of fairness (see, for example, Messick *et al.* 1985).

Huddy and Virtanen (1995) provide an interesting example of accentuation effects among Hispanic subgroups in the US. They examined affective ratings (positivity/negativity) and evaluative trait ratings made by Anglo Americans, Cuban Americans, Puerto-Rican Americans, and Mexican Americans toward their own group and each of the other three groups. The ratings of the four target groups were made in the context of a larger rating task in which respondents evaluated 15 national groups. As seen in Table 3.1a, the Latino groups saw considerably less similarity between themselves and each of the two other Latino groups than did the Anglo Americans, who, in keeping with the outgroup homogeneity principle, saw relatively few distinctions among all three Latino subgroups. At the same time, however, each Latino subgroup saw as much similarity between the two other Latino subgroups as did the Anglos.

Not surprisingly, in their affective ratings of the three specific Latino groups, Anglo Americans exhibited the ethnocentric bias so common in intergroup perceptions, evaluating all three Latino groups more negatively than their own group. More noteworthy is that each Latino group exhibited as much bias against members of the other two Latino groups as did Anglos, suggesting an attempt to buttress their own positive distinctiveness by displaying negativity toward the two other Latino subgroups (see Table 3.1b). Interestingly, the magnitude of bias against other Latino subgroups exhibited by Cuban Americans, the subgroup with the highest social class standing among the three, tended to exceed that shown by the other two Latino groups. Finally, each subgroup was more likely to regard members of the more general category

Table 3.1   Accentuation of intergroup differences among Latino subgroups

(a) *Similarity correlations pooled across affect, trait, and belief dimensions*

	Target of ratings	
	Correlations between ratings of own and other group	Correlations between ratings of Latino outgroups
Raters:		
Latino American	.29	.63
Anglo American		.72

(b) *Ethnocentric affective bias*

	Mean ratings by Latino American subgroups	Mean ratings by Anglo Americans
Target:		
Own group	4.54	3.88
Other Latino groups	3.61	3.17
(Bias)	+.93	+.71
Own group	4.54	
Anglo group	3.85	
(Bias)	+.69	

Source: Adapted from Huddy and Virtanen (1995)

label "Hispanic" as similar to themselves and dissimilar to the other two subgroups, thereby seemingly appropriating the more generic term "Hispanic" for their own Latino subgroup.

In this example, then, the accentuation effects shown by Latino subgroups in their evaluations of each other were as strong as those exhibited by white Americans when evaluating either Hispanics in general or specific Latino subgroups. These findings are interesting in their suggestion of a strong motivation for positive distinctiveness on the part of the three lower status subgroups. For each Latino subgroup this motivated bias was exhibited at the expense of the other Latino subgroups, even though they shared with them not only language, religion, and other cultural features, but also, a relatively disadvantaged state within the broader US society.

The effects of arousal and mood on responses toward the outgroup

Physiological arousal can tax cognitive resources. In the early days of experimental psychology, Easterbrook (1959) proposed that an increase in arousal causes selective attention toward the most salient cues in a situation. This restricted, selective attention has the effect of altering interpretation of the total situation. In social situations, arousal and the concomitant narrowing of attentional focus can increase reliance on stereotypes, which may lead one toward negatively biased inferences based on incomplete information.

Imagine, for instance, that two university friends are walking toward campus to take an exam. Eddie is in a neutral mood, but Steve is in a highly aroused state because he does not feel well prepared for the important exam he is about to take. As they walk, a black man, running quickly, bumps Steve slightly. A moment later the friends hear the sound of a police siren. Two policemen approach and explain that a silent burglar alarm has sounded in the building the friends have just passed. They query the two, asking if they saw anything suspicious. Steve, who is agitated, tells the policemen of the black man, wearing dark clothing, who ran by a moment earlier. Focusing on this limited information, the policemen look to Eddie for corroboration. Recall, however, that Eddie was unaroused and therefore had more cognitive resources for noticing not only the central cues relevant to the man and the situation, but also the details, or the peripheral cues. He remembers that the man was wearing a navy-blue business suit and tie, was carrying an expensive-looking attaché case, and seemingly was running to catch a bus that had just pulled away before he could reach the bus stop. Eddie's unaroused (or neutral) state allowed him to attend more carefully, and to process and remember the peripheral cues that, in this case, might have considerably lessened the suspicions of the police.

Experiments show that the source of the arousal – whether it is physical or psychological – is irrelevant in producing these effects. Stereotypic processing can be increased even from arousal that is produced by recent physical exertion. Kim and Baron (1988) demonstrated this in an experiment involving stereotypes of occupational groups. Sets of adjectives were selected that were rated as characteristic of each of three occupations: librarians (e.g. practical, wise, serious, studious), stewardesses, and waitresses.

Using these adjectives, the researchers created sentences, each of which described a woman by her first name, gave her occupation, and gave two of the trait adjectives. No two adjectives were paired together more than once, nor were two adjectives that had been judged as characteristic of the same occupation paired together in any one sentence. Thus a typical sentence read: "Sue, a librarian, is wise and stylish." Note that "wise" is part of the librarian stereotype, but "stylish" is part of the stewardess stereotype.

Level of physiological arousal was manipulated in this experiment by having half of the subjects exercise on a stationary bicycle prior to reading the sentences. Then all subjects read the full set of sentences (presented for five seconds each with a slide projector) and were asked to estimate the frequency with which adjective-occupation pairs occurred within the sentences. Those in the high arousal condition were not only less accurate in their frequency estimates of the adjective-occupation pairs that were presented, but in their errors they overestimated the frequency of occupation-consistent (i.e. stereotypic) traits.

Incidental affect and affective priming

Arousal may be a general state, as when produced by physical exercise, but arousal is also a concomitant of specific emotional states, such as happiness, disgust, anger, sadness, or anxiety. Bodenhausen (1993) distinguished between two sources of emotional arousal that can be elicited in intergroup situations. When emotional responses are aroused directly by actual or anticipated contact with outgroup members, the arousal is labeled *integral affect*, because it is inherent in the contact situation itself. When the source of emotional arousal is not directly related to the intergroup contact but caused instead by other factors that are unrelated to category membership, it is termed *incidental affect*. Emotional arousal of both types has been found to influence the course of intergroup interactions.

Incidental affect biases subsequent or concurrent ingroup–outgroup interactions by limiting the cognitive resources that are available in the situation. In addition, however, the valence (positive or negative) of the affect is important. Numerous studies provide evidence of "affective priming," or mood-congruency effects in which mood facilitates responses that match the valence of one's mood and inhibit those that oppose it in valence. For instance, when judging an interviewee in a videotaped interview between an employer and a job applicant, subjects induced to be happy – as compared to those made sad – will see more positive and more skilled behaviors, but also fewer negative and unskilled behaviors. These effects are particularly consistent in studies of social judgments (Forgas 1990; Bower 1991), and in the learning of mood-congruent information (Bower 1981).

In accord with affective priming effects, if one approaches a social interaction while in a bad mood, attention toward negative (as opposed to neutral or positive) aspects of the situation is increased (Higgins and King 1981), and more negative information is noticed, processed, and available to influence the valence of attributions and actions. Stereotypes about outgroups most often are predominantly negative, and consequently lead to expectations that are likely to organize our interaction with a previously unknown member of the outgroup in ways that promote hostility, rejection, or conflict. Our negative stereotypes will lead us to expect negative behaviors from that stranger. Thus it is not surprising that interactions with an outgroup member can often go badly. What is important with respect to the role of incidental negative affect, however, is that even if that stranger approaches us with positive intentions, the effect of a negative mood acts to increase the likelihood that we will interpret that person's ensuing behavior as confirming our negative expectations – the friendly intention can be seen as evidence of pushiness; the inquisitive interest, as nosiness; or the reserved and tactful approach, as snobbishness and insincerity. In other words, whatever the form that the truly positive intentions of the outgroup stranger may take, their manifestations in his or her behavior can readily be interpreted negatively (Campbell 1967).

In addition to the effects just described, some negative mood states, such as sadness, increase attention toward self (Carlson and Miller 1988). Such inward focus further acts to limit available cognitive capacity for unbiased information processing. This means, for example, that if one is in a sad or depressed state and is evaluating in a short period of time an array of well-qualified prospective employees, each of whom presents substantial relevant background information, the information processing needed for an unbiased evaluation will be impaired. This will increase reliance on stereotypes linked to the social category memberships of the applicants.

In sum, a negative mood biases perception in two ways. First, it takes up valuable cognitive resources. This effect occurs independently from whether the evaluated individual is an ingroup or an outgroup member (Griffitt 1970; Gouaux 1971). Second, it directs attention to negative aspects of the situation. But in the case of an outgroup target, negative stereotypic schemas or views are more likely to be available and called upon when attention is occupied by one's negative mood (Stangor and Ford 1992) and, moreover, the same stereotypic trait can be evaluated more negatively when the perceiver is in a bad mood (Esses *et al.* 1994).

But what about the effects of incidental positive feeling states on perceptions of group characteristics? Though less consistent, such studies yield findings similar to those for negative feeling states. Happy subjects, too, show more evidence of stereotyping than neutral subjects, particularly with respect to negative group attributes (Isen and Daubman 1984; Mackie *et al.* 1989). If we assume that happiness primes positive feelings, why should this effect obtain? Like other forms of arousal, happiness uses precious cognitive resources. One needs to pay attention to one's good mood in order to maintain it (Wegener and Petty 1994). Again, this limits the breadth of cues that one uses in order to understand or evaluate other persons and situations. Thus, the effect is congruent with others that limit our cognitive capacity. It causes more superficial information processing and, thereby, greater reliance on categorization and stereotyping.

Integral affect

It is also important to consider the consequences of emotion that is elicited as a direct result of contact with members of the outgroup. For some outgroups, difference in and of itself is likely to invoke negative affect. That is, strangeness or unfamiliarity may produce a negative feeling state even in the absence of negative conditioning, negative affective priming, or prior negative outcomes with members of that outgroup. For example, it has been found that four- to 24-month-old white infants show more frequent anxious-avoidant responses to black, as opposed to white, strangers (Feinman 1980). Additionally, as strangers move closer to the infant, anxiety increases more if the stranger is black. In the same study these white infants showed more receptive or welcoming responses to white, as opposed to black, strangers. This and other studies suggest that a primitive type of person categorization, which is automatic and unlearned, separates persons who are similar and familiar from those who are different or strange.

The capacity of a salient outgroup to elicit negative affect and associated negative cognitions was shown in an interesting series of studies by Dovidio and his colleagues. In one study (Dovidio *et al.* 1986) white subjects saw brief flashes of the word "white," "black," or "house" on a video screen. Subjects were then asked to think about the typical black person, white person, or house. Then they were asked to indicate separately whether each adjective in a series could or could not ever truly characterize the initially presented categories. Thus, for each adjective, subjects first saw one of the three category primes and were then presented with a test adjective. The test adjectives consisted of positive and negative words that had been pretested as being stereotypically characteristic of the two racial categories. For instance, "practical" and "musical" were among the positive words for whites and blacks respectively, whereas "stubborn" and "lazy" were among the negative adjectives for each group respectively.

The speed with which the white subjects pressed a computer button indicating whether an adjective could ever be characteristic of the category showed that the cue "white" facilitated the processing of positive traits that were part of the white stereotype, whereas "black" facilitated the processing of negative traits comprising the black stereotype. These results showed that when an outgroup category is made salient, it facilitates the processing of affectively negative (but not positive) material that is consistent with the stereotype of that outgroup. In other studies Dovidio and his colleagues produced similar results (Perdue *et al.* 1990). Priming or cueing with an ingroup designator ("we") produced more positive associations than did an outgroup designator ("they"). Moreover, in some studies these effects occurred when subjects were not aware of the fact that an ingroup or outgroup designator had been presented.

As previously suggested, researchers have noted that anxiety is a frequent consequence of outgroup contact (Stephan 1992; Stephan and Stephan 1993). For example, a woman walking into a work setting comprised of six men is likely to be very aware of her own outgroup and minority status, as well as the social category distinction between herself and the others in the setting. Consequently, she is likely to be somewhat anxious. Though she may be unaware of psychological studies which show that men, in fact, do tend to interrupt speakers more frequently than do women (Eakins and Eakins 1978), she may nevertheless be sensitive to that issue. She may hold the stereotypic view that males are harsh on females in business, and fear that they will evaluate her negatively and discount her ideas. Her discomfort and anxiety may be even higher if her previous experiences with other all-male groups have also been negative. Stephan and Stephan (1985) posit that the anxiety experienced in anticipation of interaction with an outgroup member has the same cause as other types of anxiety – that is, anticipated negative outcomes for oneself.

There are several reasons why anxiety might be elicited in anticipation of, or during, intergroup contact. For instance, the ingroup member may be aware of cultural differences between self and other, as when Dutch nationals interact with Turks (Dijker 1989). Often, one does not know how to behave when confronted with such differences. When Americans interact with Japanese, they are likely to feel embarrassed about the bowing behavior of the Japanese, not having learned what is appropriate in response to it. Further, familiarity with the customs and ways of one's culture and unfamiliarity with those of the outgroup often result in judgments of moral superiority of the ingroup relative to the outgroup (Sande *et al.* 1989). This, in turn, is likely to result in feelings of mistrust regarding the intentions of the outgroup (Schopler and Insko 1992). In line with the previously discussed tendency to attribute one's own attitudes to others, this feeling of distrust is likely to be projected on to the outgroup, further augmenting existing feelings of anxiety because one assumes that if I distrust them, they too must distrust me. Additionally, as Pettigrew showed many years ago, the prejudiced behavior of whites toward blacks in the southern part of the United States was to a substantial degree a manifestation of conformity to community norms (Pettigrew 1975). Consequently, when manifesting positive behavior toward members of the outgroup, concern about ingroup rejection can be another source of anxiety.

As previously indicated, higher levels of anxiety, along with other states of affective arousal, occupy our limited cognitive resources and cause more superficial information processing. In turn, this fosters a greater reliance on stereotyping and categorization, and a less detailed and thorough view of each individual. Anxiety causes assimilation of judgments about the members of social categories, amplifying the ordinary tendency to minimize differences within categories (Stroessner and Mackie 1993; Wilder 1993a). Likewise, anxiety amplifies the characteristic tendency of accentuation of differences between categories (Wilder 1993b).

Of course, anxiety is not the only negative integral affect likely to be aroused in an intergroup context. E. Smith (1993) suggests that five specific emotions are most likely to be aroused in intergroup situations: fear, disgust, contempt, anger, and jealousy. Of these, fear and disgust can be distinguished as emotions that imply avoidance or movement away from the outgroup, whereas contempt and anger imply movement against the outgroup. Attitudes that are driven by the former emotional states are likely to have different cognitive contents and behavioral implications than attitudes that are associated with the latter forms of emotion (Kovel 1970).

The difference between the two forms of negative affect toward outgroups may be a function of the degree of conflict of interest that is perceived to exist between the outgroup and the ingroup. As perceived conflict increases, avoidant emotions such as anxiety and disgust may be replaced by active hostility and aggression. This relationship was indicated by results of a study of the attitudes of Israeli citizens towards members of an ultraorthodox sect (Struch and Schwartz 1989). Two types of intergroup attitudes were assessed, one measuring aggressive intent against the outgroup, the other measuring more conventional ingroup–outgroup evaluative ratings. The strongest predictors of ratings on the aggression measure were perceived conflicts of interests and value conflicts between the respondent's own religious group and the outgroup sect. However, these conflict measures did not predict the more traditional evaluative ratings, and these two measures of outgroup attitude were essentially uncorrelated.

Taken together, these findings suggest that outgroup status in and of itself – and in the absence of the experience of prior negative consequences or priming – induces integral affect that is negative in valence. Moreover, this process can, and often does, occur outside the scope of conscious awareness.

Aggression

In the research discussed to this point, the key dependent measures have been perceptions and evaluative judgments – not overtly hostile or harmful behavior that is exhibited in the context of face-to-face interaction. Experimental studies of aggression provide an opportunity to examine hostile behavioral effects induced by outgroup status in social interaction settings. Often, such studies have employed the *teacher–learner paradigm*, which typically proceeds as follows. Two participants enter the laboratory. Unknown to the true subject, however, the other participant is not a true subject, but a confederate of the experimenter. Allegedly the experiment concerns the effects of punishment on learning. A coin is tossed, and the subject is assigned the role of "teacher" while the confederate takes the role of "learner." The subject, as teacher, then receives instructions on how to control the duration and intensity of the electric shocks he or she will deliver to the learner when the learner makes errors. Sometimes, the subject receives a small shock from the experimenter, ostensibly "to have direct experience with the sensation," but in reality to augment the credibility of the setting. The confederate is then connected or strapped to the bogus machine and given a task to learn. The experimental instructions require the subject to deliver a shock each time the learner makes a mistake, but the subject is free to select both its intensity level (from an array of shock buttons) and the duration for which it is depressed. In this paradigm, shock intensity is interpreted as an expression of direct aggression, whereas shock duration is thought to reflect indirect aggression in that subjects receive no instruction about duration and are less aware of the degree to which they vary the duration of the shocks they apply to the learner across trials.

Factors that moderate the expression of direct and indirect aggression

Although outgroup members receive higher levels of aggression than ingroup members in some studies (e.g. Donnerstein and Donnerstein 1978), further experiments have isolated several variables that interact with group membership to affect aggressive responding. Specifically, threat of retaliation, anonymity, and the potential for future censure are key factors. Depending on the circumstance, these factors may work to either exacerbate or inhibit the expression of aggression toward outgroup members. Interestingly, however, with regard to levels of aggression expressed toward ingroup members, manipulation of these same factors often has no effect on the expression of aggression.

Threat of retaliation was manipulated in a number of studies by telling subjects at the start of the experiment that the roles of teacher and learner would be reversed after the first learning task (Donnerstein *et al.* 1972; Donnerstein and Donnerstein 1973, 1975). Whereas threat of retaliation had little effect on the expression of aggression by white subjects toward other ingroup members, when aggression toward outgroup members was measured it interacted with type of aggression expressed. Under the threat of retaliation, white male subjects expressed less direct aggression toward black males than toward ingroup members, but at the same time, they expressed higher levels of indirect aggression toward outgroup members.

Manipulating anonymity and censure produces an interaction similar to that produced by threat of retaliation (Donnerstein and Donnerstein 1973, 1978). Specifically, when the white subjects were identifiable or threatened with the potential for future censure, they expressed less direct aggression toward black targets in comparison to white targets. But, as in the retaliation studies described above, they expressed more indirect aggression. In an anonymous condition, however, these results were reversed. As with the results of previous studies, these same variables did not affect the expression of aggression toward ingroup members. Taken together, these data imply that although anti-outgroup hostility may in fact be present, it is only expressed when certain prerequisite conditions for its inhibition are absent. That is, threat of retaliation, lack of anonymity, and threat of future censure, all inhibit the direct, but not the indirect, expression of aggression toward outgroup members.

Provocation

In the studies previously discussed, you may have felt that there was a lack of correspondence with real-world situations in that people typically behave aggressively toward others after they have been attacked or provoked, or when they think another person has offended or abused them. By contrast, many experimental studies have assessed aggression in the absence of any prior or perceived provocation. Within the experimental research on aggression, however, there is a large literature that examines the effects of prior provocation. In many of these studies, the source of provocation subsequently becomes the target toward whom aggressive responding is observed. Researchers have induced such provocation by having the target, a confederate, insult the subject (Richardson *et al.* 1994) or evaluate his or her performance as poor or below standard (Baron 1972). Not surprisingly, provocation consistently increases aggression relative to that exhibited by unprovoked control subjects.

In a number of other studies, however, experimenters have imposed prior provocation that emanates from sources other than the target toward whom aggression is subsequently observed. In these studies researchers have provoked subjects by personally attacking them for poor performance in completing a task (e.g. Mosher and Proenza 1968; Caprara *et al.* 1984); or for failing to complete it within a specified time limit (e.g. Konecni and Doob 1972); by exposing the subject to frustrating events, such as an insoluble task, and thereby creating perceptions of personal inadequacy (e.g. Geen and Berkowitz 1967; Geen 1968); and by rigging failure in a competition (e.g. Burnstein and Worchel 1962). Others have induced negative affect in the absence of any personal agent or provocateur by imposing annoyances, such as being crowded in a laboratory space (e.g. Baum and Greenberg 1975); requiring subjects to put their hand in cold water (e.g. Berkowitz *et al.* 1981); filling the air with secondary cigarette smoke (e.g. Zillmann *et al.* 1981); or requiring subjects to work on a task while exposing them to loud noise played through headphones (e.g. Donnerstein and Wilson 1976). The results of these and other experiments leave little doubt that prior provocation, even when its source has virtually no connection with a subsequent target of aggression, augments aggressive responding toward that target.

As with other processes discussed above, however, it is likely that responses to a provoking event will depend on whether its source is an ingroup or outgroup member. Group members may affect the valence and intensity of attributions about the provocation and subsequent actions that may result. That is, the same act will be interpreted differently when performed by an ingroup or outgroup member. As we have previously argued, outgroup status is likely to prime negative cognitive associations and affect, and thereby increase the likelihood that an outgroup member's action will be perceived as intentional or hostile. It follows, then, that after one has been provoked by another, the level of retaliation will be higher if that other is a member of an outgroup as opposed to an ingroup. Perceptual, cognitive, and attributional processes combine such that even a trivial or accidental action by an outgroup member may elicit exaggerated negative attributions and strong negative affect which, in turn, induces aggressive responding. Conversely, when the instigating source is an ingroup member, the provoking event must be more clearly and unambiguously hostile to exceed the threshold for aggression and elicit a retaliatory response.

Baron (1979) used insult to examine the effect of provocation on the disinhibition of aggression by white subjects toward ingroup and outgroup members. Prior to their introduction to the teacher–learner paradigm, half of the subjects overheard the black or white learner, in reality a confederate of the experimenter, directly insult the subject. Although hearing a white target insult them had no effect on subjects' levels of direct or indirect aggression, as expressed through shock intensity and duration respectively, it did have a disinhibiting effect on the expression of aggression toward a black target. In addition, in the no-insult condition, subjects expressed significantly less aggression toward black targets than toward white targets. That is, when not angered, Baron's white subjects displayed a type of reverse racism wherein they expressed greater aggression toward ingroup members than toward outgroup members. When angered, the level of aggression expressed toward ingroup members did not increase significantly, but that toward outgroup members was reliably greater than that expressed in the no-insult condition.

A variation of this experiment examined the effect of provocation on aggression, but placed the subjects in a group setting in which their responses were supposedly indistinguishable from the other three members of their group (Rogers and Prentice-Dunn 1981). White male subjects were told that the shock level that each of them set for the target learner would be averaged with the levels set by three others to determine the intensity and duration of shock that would be delivered to the target, thereby making each individual subject's actions anonymous. The results of this study paralleled those of the Baron study in three ways: in the no-insult condition, less direct and indirect aggression was displayed toward the black outgroup targets than toward ingroup targets; provocation did not affect the levels of direct or indirect aggression that white subjects expressed toward ingroup targets; and lastly, provocation augmented the level of aggression expressed toward outgroup members. Unlike Baron's study, however, in the provocation condition the level of aggression expressed toward outgroup targets, whether direct or indirect, reliably exceeded that expressed toward ingroup targets (see Figure 3.2). Apparently the anonymity conferred by collective action was important. The interaction between the presence or absence of provocation and the race of the target (as an ingroup or outgroup member) emerged more strongly in the group setting. Taken together, research suggests that when people in a crowd are emotionally aroused by a provocation, both blacks (Wilson and Rogers 1975) and whites will readily aggress against outgroup targets (Miller and Dollard 1941: 218).

Displaced aggression

The studies we have just described examined retaliation, which is aggression directed against the person who is perceived to have provoked it. Although retaliation against the provocateur is a common form of aggression, sometimes aggression is instead displaced on to a target other than one who instigated the anger. This may be necessary because retaliation is feared: as, for example, when the provocateur is powerful – she is the boss and has the ability to fire you. The unavailability of the perceived cause of the provoking act may also set the stage for displaced aggression. For example, the offending person may be unavailable in the immediate environment – a hit-and-run driver left a dent in your parked car. Finally, in many instances, the source of one's annoyance is unknown, intangible, or impersonal. For example, a jackhammer pounding outside may be giving you a headache, or there has been a power failure and you have lost all the work that you have entered into your computer during the preceding hour.

When circumstances prevent direct retaliation, aggression may be redirected toward more available displacement targets (Dollard *et al.* 1939). Displaced aggression, then, is an act of harm directed at a target other than the original source of provocation. Thus previously elicited but inhibited or unexpressed anger or hostility lies dormant behaviorally, but has been primed and may persist ruminatively until some future time. Here our previous discussion of types of provocation that emanate from a source other than the

Figure 3.2   Group aggression as a function of insult and target race

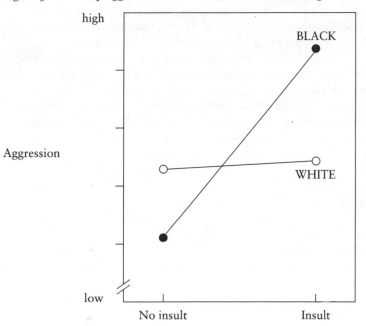

Source: adapted from Rogers and Prentice-Dunn (1981)

target of aggression is relevant. A meta-analysis (a quantitative integration and summary) of this literature shows that displaced aggression is a reliable effect (Miller and Marcus-Newhall, in press).

Of special interest here, however, is the role of triggering acts on the part of the displacement target in augmenting displaced aggression and in how the source of a triggering act moderates its effect. Although there is no research on this issue, the data and arguments we have presented in this chapter argue that even minor acts of provocation on the part of an outgroup member can be a very potent instigation for the display of displaced aggression. The cueing functions of outgroup membership and the attributional distortions that characterize the interpretation of outgroup behavior – when allied with the priming effect of a negative mood induced by a previous provocation from another source – are likely to result in stronger aggressive action. Consider, for instance, the likely result when a gang member who was just "chewed out" by his boss, comes home to hear his well-loved grandmother say "your

shoes sure look funny." Imagine, instead, the consequences of
the same remark when uttered by a rival gang member. Although
the grandmother's remark may elicit some anger, it may just as
likely be interpreted as benign, or even as teasing, but loving and
friendly attention. When uttered instead by a rival gang member
(in the same intonation) the negative cognitive and motivational
factors that are ordinarily mobilized by outgroup category membership are likely to be given explosive fueling by the mildly provocat-
ive, if not ambiguous comment. We suspect that such triggering of
displaced aggression can be seen in collective intergroup dynamics,
as well as in ingroup–outgroup interaction at the interpersonal level.

Aversive racism

In the studies described in the preceding section (Baron 1979;
Rogers and Prentice-Dunn 1981), in the no-insult conditions,
white Americans displayed less direct and indirect aggression
toward black outgroup targets than toward white ingroup targets.
In other words, this aspect of the data seems to suggest that whites'
behavior toward blacks is less negative than their behavior toward
other whites. In much of this chapter, however, we have argued
exactly the reverse, namely, that ingroup members will behave
more negatively toward outgroup members than toward members
of their own group. What can account for these results in studies
of aggression?

In our brief discussion of ambivalence/amplification (Katz and
Hass 1988; Hass et al. 1991), we outlined the complex motivations that exist between a dominant, politically powerful group
(e.g. whites in the US) and a less powerful or disadvantaged
minority group (blacks in the US). Recent survey data in the US
support the view that white Americans' attitudes toward black
Americans have become more accepting (Dovidio and Gaertner
1986); in 1989, within the National Research Council, the Committee on the Status of Black Americans concluded that "White
attitudes concerning black–white relations have moved appreci-
ably toward endorsement of principles of equal treatment..."
(Jaynes and Williams 1989: 155–6). This emphasis on egalitarian
values typically exerts pressure on members of the dominant group
to behave in a non-prejudiced manner toward members of the
disadvantaged group. However, theories of "aversive" (Gaertner

and Dovidio 1986), "modern" (McConahay and Hough 1976; McConahay 1986), "symbolic" (Sears 1988; Sears and Funk 1991), or "regressive" racism (Rogers and Prentice-Dunn 1981) argue that there is a conflict between egalitarian values and the antipathy toward outgroup members that is caused by the many processes that we have discussed, such as similarity attraction, the ultimate attribution error, the processing of and attention to stereotype-consistent information, incidental and integral affect, outgroup status as a prime for negative affect, and both outgroup homogeneity and accentuation of group differences.

Simply stated, aversive racism is the tendency of white subjects in the US to mask overt expression of prejudice toward black Americans. Among the propositions of aversive racism (Gaertner and Dovidio 1986) is that the salience of egalitarian values influences the expression of racial bias. When the salience of egalitarian values is high, there will be no overt display of racial discrimination. When, instead, it is low, discrimination will be evident. According to the model, prejudice influences behavior via an indirect process whereby the race of the other person enhances the salience of elements in a situation that would justify or rationalize a negative response to that individual.

In interactions between ingroup and outgroup members, then, egalitarian values may typically exert pressure to behave in a nonprejudiced manner. However, when there is a justifying cause that can rationalize a negative response toward anyone, in the presence of outgroup members this will legitimize negative behavior toward them. This can result in amplified negative responses and prejudice that is not recognized as such by the actor. This analysis can account for the enhanced aggression that is expressed toward outgroup targets when aggression is indirect or provoked by external provocation.

Another explanation for the consequences of ambivalence or aversive racism is that conflict of values affects resources available for cognitive processing. Devine (1989), for instance, argues that because prejudicial responses are well learned from early childhood, two processes are necessary for suppression of prejudiced behavior: the inhibition of automatically activated negative stereotypes, and the activation of "controlled information processing" that makes salient those associations that are consistent with egalitarian values. Under these conditions, an individual may be able to inhibit negative associations and behave in a manner

consistent with egalitarian values. If, however, either time or processing capacity is limited or constrained, biased behavior emerges
as a consequence of overlearned negative racial associations. This
suggests that biased behavior, even in one who sincerely embraces
egalitarianism, is not the result of prejudice, *per se*, but of "prejudice-
like" cognitive associations that are a function of efficiency in information processing.

In these models, it is the circumstance that determines the
overt expression of racial bias. Thus, to inhibit the expression of
outgroup hostility, circumstances must clearly promote the salience
of egalitarian values. Factors that serve this function include
moral and religious exhortation to extend egalitarian principles to
outgroups of all types; media emphasis on the inappropriateness
of displaying ethnocentric attitudes; and endorsement of egalitarian
attitudes by high status persons such as teachers, political and
business leaders, and parents. In effect, it is not enough simply to
suppress negative responses toward outgroups; rather, they need to
be replaced with positive value systems.

Conclusion

The idea that racial prejudice represents a motivational conflict
has led social psychologists to a renewed interest in the affective
or emotional component of attitudes toward outgroups in general.
It has long been recognized that intergroup attitudes are a complex
mixture of affective, evaluative, and cognitive responses, but recent
social psychological research has been dominated by a focus on
the cognitive component (stereotypes) to the relative exclusion of
the more emotional underpinnings of prejudice. Although feelings
and emotions toward specific outgroups are certainly connected
to beliefs about those groups, these components are conceptually
and empirically separable (Esses *et al.* 1993).

Zanna and Rempel (1988) have suggested that an attitude can
be defined as an overall evaluation of a social group that is based
on a combination of cognitive information (beliefs and stereotypes) and affective information (feelings and emotions). Attitudes
toward different groups may reflect different weightings of affective
and cognitive components. For some individuals, prejudice toward
a specific group may be primarily emotion-driven, while for other
individuals or other groups, prejudice is primarily a matter of beliefs

and values (Esses *et al.* 1993). Further, emotional states may directly affect the beliefs and evaluations associated with an outgroup.

Emotional reactions to a particular outgroup can include positive emotions (e.g. admiration, respect) as well as a range of negative emotions (e.g. fear, disgust, anxiety, and hate). In Dijker's (1987) examination of the relation between emotions and attitudes toward two minority groups in the Netherlands, although both types of emotion occurred in evaluation of the outgroups, positive emotions were more descriptive of attitudes toward one group and negative emotions were more descriptive of attitudes toward the other. Similarly, in an investigation of the relation between positive and negative emotional responses toward seven minority groups in the United States, both types of emotion were characteristic of prejudice toward these groups (Stangor *et al.* 1991: Study 1).

The emotional component of prejudice is made more complex when one realizes that positive and negative affect may be held independently (Larson and Diener 1992; Cacioppo and Berntson 1994). If positive and negative emotions are potentially independent, the reduction of extreme negative affect toward a particular outgroup does not necessarily result in increased positive affect. Recently, Pettigrew and Meertens (1995) have suggested that although "blatant" forms of prejudice against outgroups involve strong negative affect, more "subtle" forms of prejudice involve the absence of positive emotional reactions toward the outgroup, rather than the presence of negative emotions. Ultimately many forms of discrimination and bias may develop, not because outgroups are hated, but because positive affects such as admiration, sympathy, and trust are reserved for the ingroup and withheld from outgroups (Brewer, in press).

Further reading

Devine, P. G. (1989). Stereotypes and prejudice: Their automatic and controlled components. *Journal of Personality and Social Psychology*, 56, 5–18. Experiments on automatic stereotype activation and the conscious control of prejudice.

Gaertner, S. L. and Dovidio, J. F. (1986). The aversive form of racism. In J. Dovidio and S. Gaertner (eds) *Prejudice, discrimination, and racism*, pp. 61–89. Orlando, FL: Academic Press. A review of research on aversive racism and indirect expression of racial prejudice.

Pettigrew, T. F. and Meertens, R. W. (1995). Subtle and blatant prejudice in Western Europe. *European Journal of Social Psychology*, 25, 57–75. A cross-national survey study of the negative and positive affective components of prejudice.

Smith, E. R. (1993). Social identity and social emotions: Toward new conceptualizations of prejudice. In D. Mackie and D. Hamilton (eds) *Affect, cognition, and stereotyping*, pp. 297–315. San Diego, CA: Academic Press. A taxonomy of emotional responses to intergroup situations.

4 / INTERGROUP DISCR
WHAT IS JUST TO U
UNFAIR TO THEM

In 1970, high school boys in Bristol, England, took part in a series of social psychological experiments that changed dramatically the future of research on intergroup relations. The experiments, conducted by Henri Tajfel and his colleagues (Tajfel 1970; Tajfel *et al.* 1971), consisted of two phases. In the first phase, eight boys from the same high school were brought together in a lecture room and told that they would be participating in a study of visual judgment. A series of 40 slides consisting of large clusters of dots were then flashed on a screen briefly and subjects wrote down their estimates of the number of dots that appeared in each cluster. Their judgments were then collected and taken away for scoring. The researcher then explained that some people consistently overestimate the number of dots in this judgment task while others consistently underestimate the actual number.

While the dot estimates were being "scored," the boys were taken into separate rooms for the second phase of the experiment. At this point they were each assigned a code number (in order to keep their personal identity unknown to others in the session) and then told whether their total number of guesses in the dot estimation task had been among the four highest in the session (the overestimators) or among the four lowest (underestimators). In actuality, these assignments were made randomly. The dot estimation task was used simply to divide the eight participants into two distinctive categories on an arbitrary basis.

The second phase of the experiment consisted of a different decision task involving assignment of monetary rewards or penalties to other participants in the session. Every participant was given a

4.1 A choice matrix from the minimal intergroup experiments

location to:

Ingroup member	18	17	16	15	14	13	12	11	10	9	8	7	6	5
Outgroup member	5	6	7	8	9	10	11	12	13	14	15	16	17	18

Source: Tajfel (1970: 97)

booklet containing 18 pages of allocation matrices. On each page of the booklet there was a matrix consisting of a series of number pairs, as illustrated in Figure 4.1. The pairs represented alternative allocations of points (worth money), with the upper number going to the person whose group label and code number was indicated on the top row, and the bottom number going to another person whose label and code were attached to the bottom row. Each page of the booklet consisted of such a set of choices for a different pair of recipients.

Now let us consider the decision being made by participants in these experiments when they were called upon to allocate points on behalf of two other individuals. On what basis could such a decision be made? Keep in mind that the decision never affected the decision maker directly (the code numbers always referred to two participants other than the decision maker himself) and he did not know the identity of the two recipients except by code number. Under such circumstances it is generally assumed that the fairest decision rule is to allocate each recipient as close to an equal number of points as possible. In the case of the choice matrix illustrated in Figure 4.1, this would mean selecting one of the options that assigned 12 points to one and 11 to the other (choice #7 or 8).

When making allocations for individuals who belonged to the same category (i.e. both were labeled "overestimators" or both "underestimators"), participants did tend to choose the most equal point distribution. However, Tajfel and his colleagues were particularly interested in what would happen in those cases when the two target individuals belonged to different categories (i.e. one "overestimator" and one "underestimator"). In this case, one of the targets would be identified as belonging to the same category as that of the decision maker (an ingroup member) while the other would be identified as an outgroup member. Under these circumstances, category membership *did* make a difference in allocation decisions. Decision makers consistently deviated from the point of maximum fairness in order to assign *more* points to the member of their own ingroup. In the first experiment conducted by Tajfel and his colleagues, 26 out of 32 participants gave more points to ingroup targets than to outgroup targets. Rarely did they go so far as to allocate the maximum possible to the ingrouper and the minimum to the outgrouper, but they did deviate significantly from an equal distribution. In the matrix depicted in Figure 4.1, for instance, participants allocated an average of 13 points to ingroup targets and only 10 to outgroup targets.

Discrimination in the minimal intergroup situation

The behavior of the decision makers in the Tajfel experiments illustrates *intergroup discrimination*. Fellow participants were treated differently by the decision makers on the basis of their group membership alone. Apparently allocators felt justified in making decisions that discriminated in favor of ingroup members and against outgroup members, even though they did not know anything about the individuals personally. Since 1970, this finding has been replicated in many experiments using different types of allocation matrices and different bases of group categorization (Brewer 1979; Turner 1981; Diehl 1990; Mullen *et al.* 1992a).

The results of the original Tajfel experiments surprised social psychologists because social discrimination was exhibited on such an arbitrary basis. The experimental procedures involve what is called a *minimal intergroup situation*. Participants are classified into separate categories that have no prior meaning (before coming to the research setting, students had never heard of "overestimators" and "underestimators"). Further, category members are unknown to each other; there is no group interaction, no history of intergroup conflict; and participants have no self-interest in the allocations they make. Yet they make decisions that discriminate in favor of members of one category over the other.

Prior to the publication of these experiments, most social psychologists had assumed that such discrimination was the result of existing prejudice and hostility that developed over time in the course of intergroup relations. Now we know that intergroup discrimination can be produced by mere categorization into separate groups, in the absence of any history of intergroup contact or conflict. This discovery not only had a profound effect on theories of intergroup behavior, it also had important methodological implications. More than had ever been realized before, it became clear that important intergroup processes could be studied in the laboratory under experimentally controlled conditions. This greatly enhanced social psychologists' ability to test theories about the processes underlying intergroup discrimination.

Discrimination and the rules of fairness

The thing that is most surprising about the results of the Tajfel experiments is that participants were willing to allocate rewards in a way that favored one individual (an ingroup member) over another (an outgroup member) without any apparent justification for the inequality. The fact that point allocations in the minimal intergroup situation deviate from equal distribution suggests that ingroup–outgroup distinctions alter concepts of what is "fair" or "just" (Messick *et al.* 1985; Messé *et al.* 1986; Platow *et al.* 1990).

Equality as a rule of fairness assumes that individuals are the same in all relevant respects and hence deserve the same outcomes. Other rules of fairness take individual differences into account in determining outcome distributions. The rule of equity, for instance, holds that individuals should receive outcomes proportional to their inputs (Walster *et al.* 1978). Those who contribute more in terms of abilities or efforts should also receive more, according to the principle of equity. One explanation for the presence of ingroup favoritism in the minimal intergroup situation is that participants assume that members of their own group are higher in ability or aptitude than members of the outgroup (an interesting form of ingroup bias in its own right). Differences in competence provide one justification for awarding more points to some individuals than others. When groups actually do differ in status or power, the tendency to discriminate in favor of the ingroup is especially strong for members of the higher status or dominant group (Sachdev and Bourhis 1991).

To test the influence of equity considerations in intergroup allocations, some experiments have given participants explicit information about individual differences in performance or con-

Table 4.1 Studies of equity in intergroup allocation

	Differential allocation to more productive worker	
	More productive worker = ingroup member	More productive worker = outgroup member
Ancok and Chertkoff (1983)	+1.53	+1.00
Ng (1984)	+3.63	−0.53
Lerner and Grant (1990)	+3.40	+2.00

tribution at the time allocations are made (Ancok and Chertkoff 1983; Ng 1984; Lerner and Grant 1990). Participants are first divided into two categories and then take part in a task which earns money for the group as a whole. At the end of the experiment they are given the opportunity to distribute part of the earnings between two other members of the group. According to feedback provided about individual contributions to the group task, one of these members was more productive than the other. When the category identity of the two members is not known, participants typically make an allocation in line with equity principles – the more productive member is allocated more points than the less productive member. When the two group members belong to different social categories, however, the allocation rule is altered. If the more productive individual also happens to be a member of the decision maker's own ingroup, even more is allocated to that individual. The principle of equity is used as a justification for enhancing the ingroup member's outcomes.

But what happens if the ingroup member is *less* productive than the outgroup member? Does the rule of equity still apply? Apparently not, because in this case participants tend to make more equal allocations between the productive outgroup member and the less productive ingroup member (see Table 4.1). Which rule of fairness is applied seems to be influenced by category membership. If equity can be applied to the benefit of an ingroup member, rewards are distributed differentially. However, if equity does not work to the ingroup's benefit, allocators shift toward an equality distribution rule. Ingroup bias apparently precedes selection of rules of fairness.

Implications for affirmative action

Both equity and equality are rules of fairness that refer to the distribution of outcomes that results from some system of allocation. It is clear from the findings of experimental studies of intergroup allocations that the use and interpretation of these outcome fairness rules are influenced by ingroup favoritism. When ingroup outcomes exceed those of outgroups, it is apparently easy for group members to justify and accept this differential in terms of some application of equity principles. However, when outcomes favor the outgroup, the same differential is likely to be evaluated as unfair and unjustified – something closer to equality seems more "fair" in this circumstance.

An interesting experimental test of differences in perceived justice was conducted by Azzi (1992) with students in the US and South Africa. Participants were given the task of dividing political power between two simulated ethnic groups that differed in size. Some subjects were given instructions to identify with, or take the position of, members of the majority group in the simulation, while others were told to identify with the minority. Those representing the majority were more likely to adopt a proportionality rule for the allocation of power and resources, with resources distributed in accord with number of individuals in each group. Those representing a minority group, on the other hand, were more likely to adopt an intergroup equality principle of distributive justice, and this was particularly true for experimental participants who themselves were members of real ethnic minorities.

It is not difficult to extrapolate from these findings why affirmative action policies should be perceived so differently by members of advantaged and disadvantaged groups. The latter are most likely to focus on the pre-existing outcome differentials that favor the outgroup unfairly, and perceive affirmative action as a mechanism for bringing the intergroup outcome distribution closer to equality. Members of the advantaged group, on the other hand, are less likely to see pre-existing differences as unfair but more likely to perceive affirmative action in terms of unfair outgroup advantage. Attitudes toward affirmative action policies are strongly influenced by whose view of fairness one accepts (Nacoste 1990).

Some possible mechanisms: mediators of ingroup bias

Once the phenomenon of ingroup bias even in minimal intergroup situations had been well established, social psychologists turned attention to theories about why the bias occurs. One implication of the minimal intergroup findings was that intergroup conflict and competition could not be accounted for solely in terms of the structural relationships between groups, as purported by *realistic group conflict theory* (Sherif 1966a, b; LeVine and Campbell 1972: Chapter 2). Instead, the search was for psychological mechanisms that might account for ingroup favoritism and competitive orientation toward outgroups even in the absence of conflict over scarce resources. Of course, these theories are not intended to explain only minimal intergroup behavior. The same psychological mechanisms are presumed to underlie ethnocentric biases and discrimination among real-world social groups, where structural factors may also play an important role.

Ethnocentric attributions

One psychological mechanism that sustains different perspectives on fairness is the attributions that are made about the causes of other persons' good or bad fortunes. If an individual performs well or succeeds because of personal effort, ability, and integrity, then he or she is perceived to deserve positive outcomes. Conversely, if failure is attributed to personal dispositions such as laziness, incompetence, or dishonesty, then poor outcomes are deserved. However, the relationship between behavior and outcomes is altered if the behavior is attributed to external factors, i.e. caused by circumstances outside the individual's control. When good performance is attributed to luck or external aid, positive outcomes are not deserved. And poor performance that was caused by bad luck or handicapping circumstances does not deserve bad outcomes.

Attributions are often made in ambiguous circumstances. It is not always clear whether behavior reflects the individual's personal dispositions or is being caused by the situation he or she is in (Jones 1979), so causal attributions are often a matter of subjective judgment. The attributions that are made for another person's behavior can be influenced by knowledge of the social group to which that individual belongs. In general, failure and negative behaviors exhibited by an outgroup member are more likely to be attributed to internal, dispositional causes than the same negative behavior by an ingroup member (where it is more likely to be attributed to external or situational causes). Conversely, positive acts and success are more likely to be attributed to internal causes for ingroup members than for members of an outgroup. As we discussed in Chapter 1, this ethnocentric pattern of attributions was labeled the "ultimate attribution error" by Pettigrew (1979), and it has been demonstrated in studies of attributions made by members of different ethnic groups, sports teams, schools, and gender categories (Hewstone 1990).

The ethnocentric attribution bias has also been demonstrated in a laboratory setting using artificial social categories. In an experiment by Weber (1994), participants were arbitrarily divided into two social categories (overestimators and underestimators – as in the minimal intergroup experiments). Following an initial phase of ingroup formation, all participants viewed a videotape depicting an interaction between teams of underestimators and overestimators. At one point in the videotape, the members of the overestimator team approach the leader of the underestimator team with a request for help. In one version of the tape, the overestimator responds positively to the request; in an alternative version, he abruptly and rudely refuses the request for help. Half of the participants saw the positive behavior version of the tape, and half saw the negative behavior version.

After viewing the video, participants were asked to give causal explanations for why the underestimator leader had behaved as he did. Consistent with the intergroup attribution bias, explanations differed depending on whether the behavior was positive or negative and whether the actor was a member of the perceiver's ingroup or an outgroup member. Specifically, the negative behavior was attributed to internal dispositions when exhibited by an outgroup member, but the same behavior was attributed to external, situational causes when the actor was an ingroup member. This tendency was particularly strong when overestimators and underestimators were in a competitive relationship with each other. In such intergroup contexts, negative or hostile behaviors on the part of the ingroup are perceived as justified by the circumstances and not indicative of any negative personality traits.

Ethnocentric attributions are a form of ingroup bias in their own right. Ingroup members are given the benefit of the doubt in ways that are not extended to outgroup individuals. These beliefs, in turn, sustain and justify other forms of intergroup discrimination. Intergroup attribution biases serve to justify differential outcomes that favor the ingroup. In effect, ingroups are credited more for successes and positive actions than are outgroups, and are less likely to be held accountable for failures or negative actions. This can explain why ingroup members are rewarded more when they outperform an outgrouper, but the same performance is not rewarded as highly when produced by an outgroup member.

The intergroup schema

In Chapter 2 we described a series of experiments conducted by Insko and his colleagues demonstrating that in situations in which either cooperation or competition is possible, people are consistently more competitive in inter*group* contexts than in interpersonal exchanges. Insko and Schopler have suggested several interesting explanations for this so-called *discontinuity effect* (Insko and Schopler 1987; Insko *et al.* 1990, 1992; Schopler and Insko 1992). The primary explanatory concept is the existence of a "group schema," learned by individuals through experience in intergroup contexts. (Interestingly, the group schema notion is not too different from an earlier idea raised by Tajfel. In describing the results of the initial minimal intergroup experiments, Tajfel (1970) speculated about a "generic norm" of intergroup behavior that prescribed outgroup competition.)

As developed by Insko and his colleagues, the group schema has at least two important components. The first is schema-based *distrust*, the learned belief or expectation that intergroup relations are competitive and therefore the outgroup is not to be trusted and the ingroup's welfare must be protected. Anticipated competition tends to create a self-fulfilling prophecy (Kelley and Stahelski 1970). When one believes that the other party has competitive intent, the only reasonable action is to compete oneself in order to avoid potential loss. Since competition begets competition, the expectancy is confirmed. Indeed, in the Insko experiments with the prisoner's dilemma game (PDG), mutual competition is the dominant response pattern in intergroup contexts. This is also consistent with Ng's (1981) equity explanation for intergroup allocation biases. Ng assumes that subjects in the minimal intergroup paradigm see themselves in a mutual control situation with an outgroup member, where each jointly determines how much the ingroup and outgroup gets. If subjects expect that the outgrouper will make a biased choice in favor of the outgroup, then the subject's own allocations will be biased toward the ingroup in order to maintain equity. In this view, ingroup bias is a strategy for maintaining equity by compensating for anticipated bias on the part of the outgroup.

Schema-based mistrust is similar to Campbell's notion of the "universal stereotype" that is attributed to all ingroups *vis-à-vis* outgroups (Campbell 1967; LeVine and Campbell 1972: Chapter 10). Whatever other content group stereotypes may contain, ingroups are believed to be trustworthy, cooperative, peaceful, and honest, while outgroups are perceived to be untrustworthy, competitive, quarrelsome, and dishonest. These stereotypes, according to Campbell (1967), have a "grain of truth" because they reflect the individual's actual experiences with ingroup and outgroup members. Since internal relations within groups are characterized by loyalty and favoritism toward fellow group members, individuals experience their own group as cooperative and friendly. However, encounters with outgroup members involve external relations, which are less cooperative and more suspicious. Hence the perception that outgroupers are quarrelsome and untrustworthy (even though those same outgroup individuals may be perfectly friendly and trusting in intragroup contexts).

In a test of the universal stereotype conducted as part of a survey study of intergroup attitudes among ethnic groups in East Africa, Brewer and Campbell (1976) found that 27 out of 30 ethnic groups rated themselves as more positive on these traits than *any* of 29 outgroups. In an experimental test of the schema-based mistrust hypothesis, Insko and colleagues (1990) found that group discussion preceding intergroup PDG play was characterized by frequent references to the potential untrustworthiness of the other group, and that there was a strong negative correlation between the amount of recorded distrust during discussion and later cooperativeness in PDG games. Further, groups more than individuals chose withdrawal from play when that option was made available, where withdrawal indicates fear that the other player will compete.

The idea that intergroup encounters are more competitive than interpersonal encounters because they are associated with learned distrust is interesting and well supported, but somewhat circular. If we approach intergroup encounters competitively because we have learned that intergroup contexts are competitive, how did the competitiveness get started in the first place? If we look at Campbell's analysis of the universal stereotype, it is clear that the trust–distrust perception is a product of ingroup favoritism rather than its cause. What this suggests is that competition and mistrust are the universal "default" expectations applied to strangers in general, but are put aside in the case of interpersonal relationships within ingroups. In other words, it is not so much that we learn to distrust outgroups but that we have come to trust the ingroup.

Furthermore, anticipated distrust does not account fully for biased allocations in favor of ingroup members. Allocations that discriminate in favor of the ingroup have been obtained even when subjects are led to expect that the outgrouper plans to make a fair/ equal allocation (Diehl 1989), and when the subject alone has full control over the final outcomes (Platow et al. 1990). These findings indicate that ingroup favoritism is motivated by something more than fear of the outgroup.

Relative gain
The second aspect of Insko's "group schema" concept is that intergroup contexts are associated with different social motives, or social values, than interpersonal exchanges. More specifically, intergroup relations entail a shift from maximizing the absolute value of one's outcomes to the goal of maximizing the relative value compared to the outcomes of another. To understand the difference between an absolute and relative gain orientation, consider the following choices among distributions of outcomes:

Outcomes to	*Choice A*	*Choice B*
Self/us	12	9
Other/them	14	7

If one's goal is to get as much as possible for oneself or one's group, then choice A is the preferred option. From this perspective, choice B makes no sense because we wind up with less value than we get from choice A. However, with choice A, the other person or group gets even more than we do. If we value our outcomes relatively, this is not satisfactory. From this perspective, choice B is the preferred outcome because our outcomes are higher than the others' outcomes. Choosing B involves sacrificing total outcomes for the sake of getting more in comparison to the other. With a relative gain orientation, all exchanges are competitive because both players cannot achieve the goal of maximizing relative gain at the same time. If I win, you lose, and vice versa.

Results of experimental studies confirm that people are more concerned with relative gain when choosing on behalf of their group than as individuals (Insko *et al.* 1992). Moreover, individuals with a strong cooperative (joint gain) value orientation do not exhibit significant allocation biases in intergroup settings (Platow *et al.* 1990). The importance of relative gain orientation as a factor in intergroup discrimination is consistent with several other explanations for ingroup bias, as discussed below.

Positive distinctiveness and self-esteem

Social identity theory, at least in its early formulations (e.g. Turner 1975; Tajfel 1978), placed a heavy emphasis on social competition for "positive distinctiveness" as the basis for ingroup bias. Biased allocations in the minimal intergroup situation were interpreted as an attempt to create a positive advantage for the ingroup over the outgroup, thus enhancing the ingroup's value in comparison to that of the outgroup. The minimal intergroup situation was particularly suited for eliciting such biases because of the absence of any pre-existing value differences between the artificially created social categories. With no positive distinctiveness already inherent in the categorization itself, subjects take advantage of the allocation task to create a positive differential in favor of the ingroup over the outgroup. This interpretation is bolstered by experiments demonstrating that discrimination is even greater when the outgroup is similar to the ingroup, rather than dissimilar on dimensions such as attitudes or interests (Diehl 1988; van Knippenberg and Ellemers 1990). Presumably there is less need for establishing positive distinctiveness relative to outgroups that are either already distinctly different or not directly comparable to one's own group.

As an explanation for ingroup bias, the positive distinctiveness hypothesis rests on two basic assumptions. The first is the assumption that group evaluation is based primarily on intergroup social comparison. On most dimensions of evaluation, the intrinsic value of the group's outcomes or position cannot be assessed except in comparison to the position of other groups on the same dimension.

Hence, the positivity of the ingroup depends on its standing relative to comparison outgroups so that relative gain orientation dominates evaluations in intergroup settings.

Second, social identity theory assumes that positive distinctiveness serves the more fundamental need for a positive self-esteem. This presumes that ingroup evaluation derived from comparisons at the intergroup level has direct implications for general self-esteem at the individual level. (See Chapter 2 for further discussion of this point.)

Research on the role of self-esteem in intergroup discrimination has taken two different directions. One line of research investigates whether discriminating in favor of ingroups and against outgroups has the effect of enhancing global self-esteem (Oakes and Turner 1980; Lemyre and Smith 1985). Other researchers have focused on the question of whether low self-esteem motivates ingroup–outgroup discrimination (Wills 1981; Crocker and Schwartz 1985; Brown *et al.* 1988).

The fact that self-esteem can be investigated both as cause and effect of discrimination leaves the overall relationship between self-esteem and ingroup bias somewhat ambiguous (Abrams and Hogg 1988; van Knippenberg and Ellemers 1993). As an effect, the relationship between discrimination and resultant self-esteem should be a positive one. As a cause, the relationship is assumed to be negative, with low self-esteem leading to more discrimination. Results of research on both directions of effect are equivocal (Abrams and Hogg 1988), but in general there is more evidence that ingroup favoritism enhances self-esteem than there is that low self-esteem individuals are more prone to discrimination than those with high self-esteem (Hogg and Abrams 1990; Crocker *et al.* 1993).

Two important distinctions in the self-esteem literature can help to clarify the otherwise murky research findings on self-esteem as a cause of intergroup discrimination. The first involves recognizing the difference between high or low self-esteem as a general, chronic characteristic of an individual's overall self-concept (*trait* self-esteem), and temporary loss or threat to self-esteem caused by experiences of embarrassment or failure (*state* self-esteem). Most of the research demonstrating a relationship between low self-esteem and discrimination has involved an experimental manipulation of temporary, state esteem. For instance, Cialdini and Richardson (1980) found that college students who had been told they performed poorly on a test of creativity rated their own university more highly and a rival university more negatively than did students who had been given more positive feedback.

In a different experimental context, Meindl and Lerner (1984) manipulated participants' self-esteem temporarily by rigging an accident. At the beginning of the experimental session, the researcher asked the participant to retrieve a missing chair from a next-door office. The chair was arranged in such a way that when the participant moved it, a large stack of computer cards spilled in disarray on the floor – computer cards that contained essential data from a graduate student's dissertation research. Following this incident, the participants (who were all English-speaking Canadians) took part in an attitude survey in which they were instructed to respond as members of the English-speaking majority in Canada. The survey included a series of questions on the "Quebec issue," in which respondents were asked to express attitudes toward French-speaking Quebec. Participants who had just experienced the esteem-lowering accident expressed significantly more negative attitudes toward their French-speaking countrymen than did those who had not had such an experience.

Such experiments support the idea that favoring ingroups or derogating outgroups relative to the ingroup may serve to restore self-esteem when it has been threatened or temporarily lowered. Moreover, recent findings in the self-esteem literature indicate that it is individuals with generally high self-esteem who are most likely to engage in self-enhancing social comparisons when their positive self-image is threatened or damaged (Taylor and Brown 1988). When self-esteem is positive and secure, high self-esteem individuals may not show much propensity to exhibit intergroup discrimination and instead value both ingroups and outgroups positively. However, when self-esteem is threatened, it is high self-esteem individuals who are most likely to respond by enhancing ingroups relative to outgroups (Brown et al. 1988). It is those who think positively of themselves in general who are most likely to be able to subscribe to the belief that their ingroup deserves favorable advantage.

A second important distinction is that between personal self-esteem and collective self-esteem (Crocker and Luhtanen 1990; Luhtanen and Crocker 1991, 1992). Most of the research linking self-esteem and intergroup discrimination has assessed self-esteem at the level of the individual, personal self-concept. Yet if one subscribes to the distinction between personal identity and social identity, it is not at all clear that self-esteem derived from evaluations of the individuated self-concept should be the same as that derived from evaluations of the ingroup. Attempts to measure collective self-esteem separately from private self-esteem indicate that global self-esteem at the two levels are positively correlated, but only moderately so (Luhtanen and Crocker 1992). It is those with high collective self-esteem who exhibit the greatest degree of intergroup discrimination when ingroup status is threatened (Crocker and Luhtanen 1990).

Intergroup status and power differentials

The importance of intergroup comparison and ingroup status highlights the fact that social groups are embedded in multigroup networks or social systems. Many such social networks are organized hierarchically, with some groups accorded more status and power than others. In fact, Sidanius (1993) has gone so far as to argue that hierarchical arrangement is a universal characteristic of all intergroup structures. Where such structural relationships do exist, psychological needs such as self-esteem and positive distinctiveness will interact with enduring power and status differences between groups to determine the degree of intergroup discrimination and the form that it takes (Hagendoorn 1995).

Experimental studies of intergroup power and status differentials that have been conducted in laboratory settings support the contention that these aspects of intergroup relationships play an important role in moderating intergroup bias and discrimination.

Status
In early versions of social identity theory, status differentials are critical to understanding intergroup relationships (Tajfel and Turner 1986). According to this view, the goal of intergroup discrimination is to achieve or maintain status differences in favor of the ingroup, a goal activated in any context where particular ingroup–outgroup distinctions are salient and attended to (Abrams 1985).

The focus on positive status differences as the motivation for intergroup discrimination raises many of the same issues as those related to self-esteem. On the one hand, high status ingroups may sustain and justify discrimination against lower status outgroups on equity grounds. On the other hand, groups that have already achieved positive status differentials should have less need for intergroup discrimination, and low status ingroups may exhibit greater discrimination in the interests of redressing unfavorable status differentials.

As with self-esteem, the findings from research on the relationship between ingroup status and intergroup discrimination are mixed. In a meta-analysis of a large number of laboratory studies, Mullen and colleagues (1992a) found that, overall, members of groups that had been accorded high status exhibit greater ingroup bias than those assigned to low status conditions (see also Sachdev and Bourhis 1987, 1991). However, this status effect is qualified by important factors related to the nature of the status differences between groups and the way in which discrimination is measured.

Discrimination on the part of high status groups is related to the relevance of the dimension of discrimination to the nature of the status differences (van Knippenberg and van Oers 1984; Mummendey and Simon 1989). In general, individuals tend to exaggerate differences between groups on those dimensions of evaluation that are favorable to their own group, but to minimize the difference when the comparison is not so favorable to the ingroup (Brewer 1979; Spears and Manstead 1989). As a consequence, there is a consistent interaction between the status of the ingroup and the status-relevance of the dimension of discrimination as determinants of ingroup bias (Mullen *et al.* 1992a).

In experimental studies of intergroup status effects, the experimenter usually introduces status differentials by providing feedback that members of one social category generally perform better than the other category on some dimension of ability, competence, or creativity. Not surprisingly, then, members of the higher status group tend to show strong ingroup bias on evaluations of competence and creativity, while the lower status group members show little or no ingroup bias on these dimensions. Similarly, members of the higher status group discriminate more in allocations to ingroup over outgroup when the allocations are seen as related to group differences in competence or ability (Sachdev and Bourhis 1987, 1991).

On other dimensions of evaluation, however, which are irrelevant to the nature of the status difference between groups, differences between high and low status groups in the degree of ingroup bias are eliminated or reversed. When evaluating groups on traits such as likeability, friendliness, and cooperativeness, members of both high and low status groups rate their ingroup more positively than the outgroup (Sachdev and Bourhis 1991). In fact, on these dimensions low status groups often show greater ingroup favoritism than high status groups (Mullen *et al.* 1992a; Brewer *et al.* 1993), possibly as compensation for unfavorable ingroup comparisons on status-relevant dimensions. When members of lower status groups are committed to their group identity, they express ingroup bias in those domains where the ingroup can be compared favorably to the higher status outgroup.

Power

In intergroup contexts, social power can be defined as the degree of control that one group has over its own fate and that of outgroups (see Jones 1972). Based on this definition, the allocation task used in the minimal intergroup experiments can be seen in terms of assignment of power to determine the outcomes (fate) of group members (Ng 1982a). When members of both groups are given allocation choices, the groups have mutual power (mutual fate control). When allocation decisions are made by members of only one of the social categories, that group has unilateral power (fate control).

In experiments where allocation power is assigned independently of status differences between groups, members of high power and equal power categories discriminate more against outgroups than members of low power groups (Sachdev and Bourhis 1985, 1991). Intergroup discrimination is particularly high on the part of high power minority groups (Sachdev and Bourhis 1991). Groups with unilateral power discriminate as much or more than groups that share mutual fate control, indicating that discrimination in favor of the ingroup is not just a defensive reaction to outgroup power (Diehl 1990).

As Sachdev and Bourhis (1991) point out, power is a necessary condition for effective discrimination. Members of low power groups may prefer allocations and status differentials that favor their ingroup, but without fate control over both ingroup and outgroup their preference will not be expressed in actual allocations. One explanation for why low status groups show little ingroup bias on status-relevant dimensions is that they feel powerless to affect or redress the status differential between groups. When low status groups are given unilateral power to control allocation outcomes, they do show significant ingroup favoritism (Cole and Bourhis 1990; Sachdev and Bourhis 1991).

Effects of instability

When experimenters assign status and power differentials to experimentally created social categories, those differences are usually assumed to be stable and legitimate. Both dominant and subordinate groups can be expected to respond differently when the status system is perceived to be unstable or subject to change. Clear-cut, stable intergroup status relations tend to reduce the salience of intergroup comparisons, but instability in the status hierarchy enhances comparison salience and intergroup discrimination on the part of both high and low status groups (Tajfel and Turner 1986; van Knippenberg and Ellemers 1990).

Tajfel and Turner (1986) distinguish three different ways in which status relationships among groups may be subject to change. These are the perceived *permeability* of group boundaries and the perceived *stability* and *legitimacy* of the status differences between groups. Permeability refers to the extent to which group members can expect to be able to move from one group to another, or shift their social identity, on an individual basis. According to social identity theory, under conditions of high permeability members of lower status groups will tend to prefer membership in the higher status outgroup and seek social mobility as a strategy for improving positive social identity (van Knippenberg and Ellemers 1993). Experimental studies have confirmed that manipulations of perceived permeability interacts with group status to affect ingroup identification. Members of low status groups express more dissatisfaction with their group membership and less ingroup preference when group boundaries are permeable rather than impermeable (Ellemers *et al.* 1988). However, when individuals could potentially change their group affiliation (high permeability), members of high status groups increase their commitment to their current group membership. Under the risk of losing their attractive group membership, high status group members express significantly stronger ingroup identification than when group membership is fixed (Ellemers *et al.* 1992).

Permeability creates instability of group membership but does not necessarily alter the status relationships between the groups as a whole. More important for social identity is the perceived stability or security of the status or dominance hierarchy itself (Tajfel and Turner 1986; Sidanius 1993; van Knippenberg and Ellemers 1993). When status differentials are perceived to be unstable or illegitimate, members of lower status groups exhibit significantly stronger ingroup identification than when status relationships are stable (Caddick 1982; Ellemers *et al.* 1990). Although perceived injustice at the personal level often motivates individuals to dissociate from low status ingroups, perceived collective injustice enhances group identification and efforts to improve the status position of the group as a whole (Taylor *et al.* 1987; Wright *et al.* 1990; Ellemers *et al.* 1993).

At the same time, perceived instability of the status hierarchy threatens the positive distinctiveness of high status groups. In experiments manipulating both group size and group status, discrimination in intergroup allocations is particularly high for minority high status groups (Mullen *et al.* 1992a). Sachdev and Bourhis (1991) argue that this is because when the dominant group is in the minority, the status structure is inherently more unstable than when the majority is dominant. Secure status differentials may reduce the salience of intergroup comparisons and discrimination, but insecurity heightens the motivation to maintain status distinctions on the part of high status group members. Thus conditions of social change increase the motivation for intergroup discrimination for groups in all positions of the dominance hierarchy.

Reverse discrimination and outgroup bias

Although discrimination that favors the ingroup over outgroups is by far the dominant pattern in intergroup relations, the existence of power and status differentials between groups provides the context in which outgroup bias can also occur. Discrimination that favors an outgroup over the ingroup is particularly interesting because it seems to violate the universality of ethnocentric bias and the drive for positive distinctiveness (Hinkle and Brown 1990).

Outgroup bias is most frequently discussed in connection with members of low status or disadvantaged groups. In both experimental and field studies, low status groups have been found not only to exhibit less ingroup bias than high status groups but sometimes to favor the outgroup over the ingroup (Mullen *et al.* 1992a). Examined more closely, however, this effect is found to occur almost exclusively on status-relevant dimensions of evaluation (Mullen *et al.* 1992a; Brewer *et al.* 1993). Considering this factor, the effect should probably not be labeled a "bias" at all. Instead it reflects acknowledgment of outgroup superiority on consensually defined status dimensions. To the extent that members of low status ingroups minimize the degree of outgroup superiority, this minimal outgroup discrimination can be a form of ingroup bias (Brewer and Campbell 1976). Further, when consensual support for status differences between groups is removed (when they are perceived to be unstable and illegitimate), outgroup bias on the part of low status groups disappears, even on status-relevant measures (Turner and Brown 1978).

As an indicator of ingroup identification, outgroup favoritism on status-relevant dimensions on the part of low status group members is ambiguous. On the one hand, it may reflect dissociation from the low status ingroup and true preference for and identification with the higher status outgroup (as discussed earlier in the case of permeable intergroup boundaries). On the other hand, it may simply reflect a strategic response to the dominant group in the face of secure status and power differentials. What has to be looked at is how low status group members evaluate ingroup and outgroup on status-irrelevant dimensions. If members are dissociated from their ingroup and seeking social mobility, outgroup preference should be exhibited on all dimensions. If outgroup favoritism is strategic, it should be limited to status-relevant dimensions while members express ingroup identification and favoritism on other measures. Most often, low status ingroups do show ingroup bias on status-irrelevant dimensions (Mullen et al. 1992a; Brewer et al. 1993), but this is moderated by the perception of permeability of intergroup boundaries (Ellemers et al. 1988).

Further supporting the strategic explanation of outgroup favoritism is the finding that relative bias on status-relevant and status-irrelevant dimensions is reversed on the part of high status group members. When status differentials are secure and legitimate, high status groups show most ingroup bias on status-relevant measures and less ingroup preference – and sometimes outgroup favoritism – on irrelevant dimensions. When outgroup favoritism is exhibited by members of high status, dominant groups, it is referred to as "reverse discrimination," suggesting that it is motivated by a desire to compensate for existing status inequities.

In some cases, reverse discrimination may reflect a value conflict between preservation of status differentials that favor the ingroup on the one hand, and egalitarian values on the other. The more a behavior is recognized as discriminatory, the more a member of an egalitarian society will "bend over backwards" *not* to exhibit such behavior toward members of a disadvantaged group (Dutton 1973). When individuals who wish to believe they are unprejudiced are made aware of discriminatory behavior, they deliberately avoid it, sometimes demonstrating reverse discrimination in the process.

This is well illustrated by the results of a study by Dutton and Lake (1973) in which white students who rated themselves as not racially prejudiced took part in what they believed to be an experiment on autonomic responses. In the course of the experiment, electrodermal activity and pulse rate of the participant was allegedly monitored as they watched a series of slides of social scenes, which included some scenes of interracial interactions. Feedback on their autonomic response was provided to participants as they viewed each slide, (spuriously) indicating the degree of negative arousal they experienced in response to each. For half of the participants, the false feedback provided in response to the interracial scenes was neutral, indicating no negative arousal. But for the remaining viewers, the feedback indicated they were experiencing high arousal, suggesting that they had unconscious racial prejudice.

When participants had completed this experiment, the researchers arranged that they would be approached as they left the laboratory by a black or a white panhandler who requested spare change for food. Participants' response to this request was significantly affected by the race of the confederate and the feedback they had just received. Those who had received neutral feedback about their responses to interracial scenes were somewhat more likely to help and to give more money to a white than a black panhandler. But when students had been threatened by evidence of their own prejudice, their reactions were reversed and they gave significantly more to the black than to the white confederate (see Figure 4.2). By the same token, when members of high status groups give favorable ratings to low status groups on evaluations unrelated to the status differential, they may be doing so to avoid seeing themselves as prejudiced or discriminatory.

Reverse discrimination on the part of high status group members may also be a case of a more general "magnanimity" effect studied by Mummendey and her colleagues (e.g. Mummendey and Schreiber 1983, 1984; Mummendey and Simon 1989). Results of this research indicate that social groups seek positive distinctiveness on dimensions that are defined as important to ingroup identity and differentiation from outgroups. Once favorable comparisons have

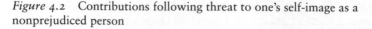

Figure 4.2   Contributions following threat to one's self-image as a nonprejudiced person

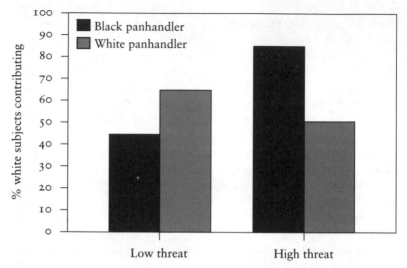

Source: Dutton and Lake (1973)

been achieved on important dimensions, ingroup bias is less likely to be exhibited on unimportant dimensions. Outgroup favoritism (magnanimity) is most likely to be displayed on dimensions of comparison that are important to the outgroup, but unimportant to the ingroup (Mummendey and Schreiber 1984; Mummendey and Simon 1989). This strategy allows both groups to be seen as "better," just in different ways. (Of course, this does not work so well for dimensions that are important to *both* groups.)

Mummendey and Schreiber (1984) point out that biases which favor the outgroup in unimportant comparisons may be an indirect or subtle form of justifying ingroup favoritism on important dimensions. Such magnanimity may be a particularly important strategy for high status groups as a form of appeasement of lower status groups, in the interests of preserving the stability of the overall status hierarchy (Sidanius 1993). When power of the dominant group is reduced or threatened, high status groups exhibit much less intergroup discrimination (Ng 1982b; Sachdev and Bourhis 1991), possibly to avoid further instability of status relationships.

The initial experiments with the minimal intergroup situation demonstrated that ingroup–outgroup categorization alone can produce intergroup discrimination, even in the absence of pre-existing structural relationships between the groups. However, the experiments reviewed in these last sections indicate that the degree of ingroup bias, or the form that it takes, is clearly influenced by the introduction of meaningful differences between groups in resources, status, or power. When these contextual factors are brought into play, the expression of ingroup bias may reflect strategic considerations, as well as perceptual and emotional processes (Ellemers 1993).

Figure 4.3 provides a schematic representation of variations in the degree and direction of intergroup discrimination as a function of status differences between ingroup and outgroup, and the perceived stability of those status relationships. The expression of ingroup bias depicted for each condition represents the interaction between ethnocentric preferences and loyalty to the ingroup, on the one hand, and strategic considerations dictated by the group's position in the dominance hierarchy, on the other.

Social status and collective movements

Research on status and power differentials between social groups gives rise to questions about when and how members of a social category – particularly members of low status or relatively disadvantaged social groups – will engage in collective action to change the existing status relationships within a given society. Theories of social identity, social comparison, and relative deprivation (see Chapter 1) all suggest that members of lower status groups will be discontented with the resources and valuation attached to their collective identity and will be motivated toward social change. Yet it seems to take a great deal more than perceived discrepancies and status differentials to mobilize collective action.

In reviewing the options available to members of low status social categories for achieving positive distinctiveness, Tajfel and Turner (1986) distinguished three different avenues of responding to negative social identity, each with different implications for collective movements:

1 *Individual mobility* – with this option, individuals dissociate themselves from the lower status ingroup and seek identification with the higher status outgroup. This route to achieving positive

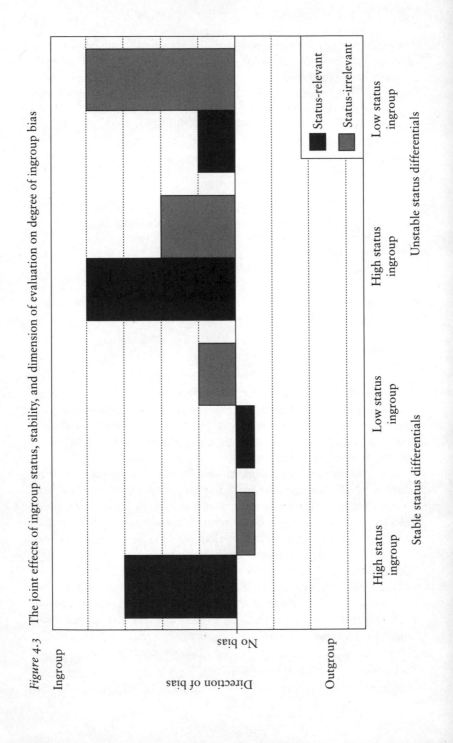

Figure 4.3 The joint effects of ingroup status, stability, and dimension of evaluation on degree of ingroup bias

social identity is most likely in social systems characterized by permeability of group boundaries and high opportunity for upward social mobility.

2 *Social creativity* – group members may achieve positive distinctiveness by redefining the bases of intergroup comparison, choosing new dimensions on which the ingroup can be assigned higher values than relevant outgroups, or changing the valuation attached to existing comparisons. The "black is beautiful" movement in the United States is an example of this latter strategy. This option essentially leaves the social relationships between groups unchanged, but alters the implications for group self-esteem.

3 *Social competition* – finally, low status group members may seek to change the structure of intergroup dominance and status differentials by engaging in direct competition with higher status outgroups. The research on instability and legitimacy reviewed above suggests some of the conditions under which the motivation for social change will be aroused. However, there are a number of psychological barriers that seem to work against collective mobilization for social change, even under conditions where relative disadvantage is evident at the intergroup level.

The perception of illegitimate relative disadvantage depends on individuals making comparisons at the intergroup rather than interpersonal levels. When personal identities, rather than social identities, are made salient, individuals are less likely to perceive relative disadvantage or to engage in collective action (Kawakami and Dion 1993).

In a conceptual review of the psychology of "entitlement," Major (1994) outlined three important factors that influence the choice of targets of comparison for members of disadvantaged groups. First is the proximity or availability of comparison groups in the immediate environment. When social categories are geographically or occupationally segregated (as is the case in most status-differentiated systems), intergroup comparisons are less salient than intragroup comparisons within the disadvantaged group itself. A second factor is the preference for making comparisons with similar others, those who are perceived as relevant targets of comparison for purposes of self-evaluation. The greater the status dissimilarity between one's own social category and outgroup categories, the less relevant comparisons between the self and members of those categories are likely to be. Finally, comparison targets are influenced by the motivation underlying social comparison in the first place. To the extent that individuals are motivated to achieve positive social comparisons, they will avoid contrasting themselves with those much more advantaged than themselves and prefer comparisons with less advantaged others. All of these factors converge to bias disadvantaged group members toward interpersonal, intragroup social comparisons rather than intergroup comparisons with better-off outgroups.

Another important factor in motivating social change is the availability of perceived "social mobility" as an alternative mechanism for achieving positive social status. If members of disadvantaged social groups believe that they have the possibility of moving, individually, into higher status categories, the motivation for collective action may be diffused. Of particular importance here is the potential role of "tokenism" as a subtle but powerful force in maintaining status structures. Even a small number of highly visible representatives of disadvantaged categories who "make it" into the advantaged statuses may preserve the perception of social mobility as a viable option. The impact of token representation on group behavior has been demonstrated in laboratory experiments by Wright and colleagues (1990).

In order to study the effects of tokenism in a laboratory context, Wright and his colleagues first developed a framework for categorizing the possible responses available to members of a disadvantaged group and then designed an experimental paradigm to determine which responses were most likely to be chosen. The response alternatives included five broad categories of behavior:

1 acceptance of the disadvantaged position
2 attempting individual upward mobility through normative means
3 individual counternormative actions
4 collective actions through normative means and
5 counternormative collective action.

Participants in the experiment were placed in a decision-making group with initially low status, but with the promise that performance on the decision-making task could potentially earn them "promotion" to the higher status category. (Members of the high status group were eligible for participation in a $300 lottery, while those in the low status group were relegated to chances of winning a $30 lottery.) Participants were then given a decision-making test, and feedback on the results of the test was used to create different experimental conditions. Of particular interest were conditions in which the subject's performance was allegedly sufficient to qualify for the high status category, but where access to entry in that category was restricted. In the "closed" condition, participants were told that a panel of high status group members had decided not to allow any of the low status group into membership, regardless of performance. In the "partially closed" condition, participants were told that 30 percent of the qualified low status group members would be admitted, and the subject him- or herself was denied admission. Finally, in the "token" condition, only 2 percent of the low status category members were permitted access to the high status group.

After receiving this information on the basis of their being denied access to the high status category, subjects were asked to rate their preferences among the five response options designated by the researchers. Available options were:

1 accept the decision
2 write an individual protest
3 request an individual retest
4 request a retest for the whole group or
5 organize a collective protest.

Participants in the partially closed condition responded to their disadvantage by accepting the outcome or seeking individual mobility (the personal retest). By contrast, those in the closed condition were most likely to endorse collective action. However, subjects in the "token" condition did not seek collective means of redress. Instead, they were more likely to prefer individual action, either normative or counternormative, that did not involve collective mobilization.

Results such as these support the idea that it takes more than the perception of unfair disadvantage at the group level to motivate collective movements (Gurin et al. 1980). A more elaborate theory of the psychological and structural conditions required for collective behavior is the five-stage model of intergroup relations developed by Taylor and McKirnan (1984; Taylor and Moghaddam 1994). The stages of the model are outlined in Figure 4.4. Note that although the model starts with recognition of stratified intergroup relations, it suggests that members of the disadvantaged strata (particularly the élite representatives of those groups) must

Figure 4.4   The five-stage model of collective behavior

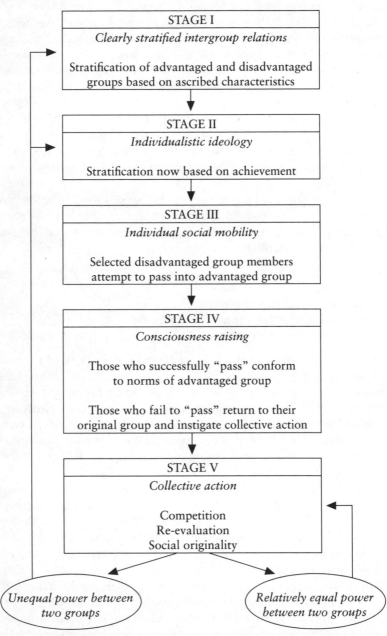

Source: Taylor and Moghaddam (1994: 142), reprinted by permission of
Greenwood Publishing Group, Inc. copyright 1994.

move through various individualistic orientations before the stages of consciousness-raising and collective action are reached.

The five-stage model integrates aspects of social identity theory with research on collective movements to describe conditions under which intergroup comparisons, perceptions of social justice, and the need for positive distinctiveness will converge to lead members of disadvantaged groups to seek social change. As discussed previously in this chapter, however, members of advantaged social categories are likely to respond to collective mobilization that threatens existing status structures with increased social identification as well. Thus, the conditions of social change are also those most likely to engender intergroup conflict, distrust, and heightened discrimination.

Summary

In this chapter we have reviewed the effects of intergroup comparison on attitudes and behavior toward ingroup and outgroup members. Overall, the results of research in this area suggest that making comparisons between salient groups enhances social competition, relative deprivation, and social instability – all factors that contribute to intergroup discrimination and conflict. In the following chapter we shift from a focus on causes of intergroup conflict to social psychological research directed toward its reduction.

Further reading

Abrams, D. and Hogg, M. A. (1988). Comments on the motivational status of self-esteem in social identity and intergroup discrimination. *European Journal of Social Psychology*, 18, 317–34. A review and critique of the role of self-esteem as an explanation for intergroup discrimination.

Brewer, M. B. (1979). In-group bias in the minimal intergroup situation: A cognitive-motivational analysis. *Psychological Bulletin*, 86, 307–24. A review of the early experimental studies employing the minimal intergroup situation.

Schopler, J. and Insko, C. A. (1992). The discontinuity effect in interpersonal and intergroup relations: Generality and mediation. In W. Stroebe and M. Hewstone (eds) *European review of social psychology*, Vol. 3, pp. 121–51. Chichester, England: John Wiley. A review of the research documenting the difference in competitive orientation evidenced in interpersonal compared to intergroup situations.

Tajfel, H. (1970). Experiments in intergroup discrimination. *Scientific American*, 223(2), 96–102. The original report of ingroup bias in the minimal intergroup situation.

Taylor, D. M. and Moghaddam, F. M. (1994). *Theories of intergroup relations: International social psychological perspectives*. London: Praeger. A comprehensive review of theories of intergroup conflict and collective action.

5 / INTERGROUP CONTACT, COOPERATION, AND COMPETITION: DOES TOGETHERNESS MAKE FRIENDS?

> See that man over there?
> Yes.
> Well, I hate him.
> But you don't know him.
> That's why I hate him.
>
> (Allport 1954: 265)

This little parable from Allport's 1954 book was intended to illustrate the idea that lack of familiarity with others can breed hostility and contempt. Mutual avoidance precludes opportunities for acquiring information that might disconfirm perceptions of the other's motives and character, thus promoting what Newcomb (1947) called "autistic hostility." Misperceptions and distrust between groups are also fed by lack of contact between members of different social categories. Hostile groups tend to maintain high social distance, avoiding interactions with outgroup members and perpetuating a cycle of further hostility and avoidance.

Intergroup contact: the social psychology of desegregation

According to Allport, this cycle captures the reasoning behind the so-called "contact hypothesis" of intergroup relations. If ignorance and unfamiliarity promote hostility, then opportunities for personal contact between members of opposing groups should reduce hostility by increasing mutual knowledge and acquaintance.

This idea played an important role in shaping desegregation policies in the United States.

When the US Supreme Court agreed to review the case of *Brown v. Board of Education of Topeka* in 1953, it had among the documents in the case a paper entitled "The effects of segregation and the consequences of desegregation: A social science statement" which was submitted as an appendix to the plaintiff's legal briefs. The statement had been drafted by social psychologists Isidor Chein, Kenneth B. Clark, and Stuart Cook, and was signed by 32 social scientists, including anthropologists, psychologists, and sociologists who were experts in race relations.

At the time, 17 states in the US either required or permitted local school districts to provide segregated schooling for black and white children. Until 1953, the Supreme Court had accepted the notion that "separate but equal" facilities for schoolchildren of different races did not violate Fourteenth Amendment rights to equal protection under the law. The *Brown* case challenged that notion. The Social Science Statement focused on psychological and social research documentation of the negative effects of legally sanctioned segregation on the self-esteem of black children, and the perpetuation of prejudice and negative stereotypes. The statement also made some recommendations regarding the potentially positive effects of desegregation, citing field research on desegregation in public housing, employment, and military units to support the conclusion that *under the right conditions* desegregation could promote positive intergroup relations and reduce unfavorable attitudes (e.g. Deutsch and Collins 1951).

When the Supreme Court rendered its decision in the case in 1954 it reversed the "separate but equal" doctrine and ruled that segregated schooling was unconstitutional. We have only indirect evidence that the Social Science Statement influenced this opinion, but some of the wording justifying the decision resembles arguments presented in the statement (Cook 1984). The opinion read in part:

> To separate them from others of similar age and qualifications solely because of their race generates a feeling of inferiority as to their status in the community that may affect their hearts and minds in a way unlikely ever to be undone ... Segregation of white and colored children in public schools has a detrimental effect upon the colored children. The impact is greater when

it has the sanction of the law; for the policy of separating the races is usually interpreted as denoting the inferiority of the Negro group. A sense of inferiority affects the motivation of a child to learn. Segregation with the sanction of law, therefore, has a tendency to retard the educational and mental development of Negro children and to deprive them of some of the benefits they would receive in a racially integrated school system. Whatever may have been the extent of psychological knowledge at the time of *Plessy v. Ferguson*, this finding is amply supported by modern authority...

(*Brown v. Board of Education*, 1954)

Some qualifying conditions

Of course, social scientists were not so naïve as to believe that physical proximity alone would be sufficient to eliminate intergroup conflict and these negative effects of segregation. The contact hypothesis has been carefully qualified to specify the conditions under which intergroup contact should promote positive relations (Amir 1969). The conditions that are expected to influence the effectiveness of personal contact as a method of reducing intergroup hostility were most recently summarized by Cook (1985). According to his review, contact can produce favorable attitudes when:

1 the situation promotes *equal status* interactions between members of the social groups
2 the interaction encourages behaviors that *disconfirm stereotypes* that the groups hold of each other
3 *cooperative interdependence* among members of both groups is involved
4 the situation must have high "acquaintance potential," promoting *intimate contact* between participants and
5 the *social norms* in the situation must be perceived as favoring intergroup acceptance.

One way to understand the conditions associated with the contact hypothesis is to think of it as an application of the principles of *dissonance theory* (Festinger 1957). Dissonance theory suggests that an effective way to change people's attitudes is to first change their behavior. Avoidance and social distance from members of specific groups are forms of negative social behavior that are consistent with hostile attitudes and distrust. If individuals with such negative attitudes find themselves in situations in which they engage in positive social interactions with members of the despised group, their behavior is inconsistent with their attitudes toward the group as a whole. It is just this sort of inconsistency that dissonance theory predicts will result in changes of attitudes to justify the new behavior (Leippe and Eisenstadt 1994). However, contact alone does not guarantee that positive interactions will occur. The contact situation must be structured in a way that promotes positive social behavior without coercion if dissonance-induced attitude change is to take place.

Robbers Cave: a classic experiment in intergroup relations

A clear demonstration that contact alone is not sufficient to reduce intergroup conflict was obtained in a classic field study conducted by Muzafer Sherif and his colleagues in the summer of 1954 (Sherif *et al.* 1961; Sherif 1966b). At that time, 22 eleven-year-old boys arrived by bus at a campsite in Robbers Cave, Oklahoma, to participate in a three-week summer camp session. The boys, all from white, middle-class backgrounds, were unaware that their camping experience would be part of a series of field studies conducted by social psychologist Muzafer Sherif and his colleagues to test their theory of intergroup conflict and conflict reduction.

Before beginning the summer camp session, the boys (who were all previously unacquainted) were arbitrarily divided into two subgroups. The two groups arrived at the camp on separate buses and were settled into cabins at a considerable distance from each other. For the first week of the session, contact between the two groups was prevented. During this time, the members of each group engaged in cooperative activities that contributed to group formation. To further the development of group identity, the boys were encouraged to adopt a group name. One group chose to call themselves the "Rattlers;" the other became the "Eagles."

When contact between the two groups did occur, beginning in the second week, it was under conditions of intergroup competition, primarily in the form of competitive sports events. But the hostilities that ensued extended well beyond the playing field. After being defeated in one game, for instance, the Eagles burned a banner left behind by the Rattlers. The next morning, the Rattlers seized an Eagles flag, and from that point on, raids on each other's campsites were frequent, along with namecalling and fist fights. Conversations and the content of posters drawn by group members documented highly derogatory images of the other group. By the end of this stage, cohesiveness within groups had increased, but both groups expressed strong preferences not to have any further contact with the other group, even if it meant foregoing pleasant activities such as movies if members of the other group were to be present.

At this point, the researchers had succeeded in demonstrating that groups with no cultural, physical, or status differences between them, composed of boys selected for good psychological adjustment and sociability, could become warring factions based on the presence of competing group interests alone. The competition that had been introduced was a "zero-sum" situation – one group's win was always the other group's loss. Once the groups had experienced this form of competition on the playing field, they continued to define all further intergroup interactions in zero-sum terms.

Having created two rival groups with hostile attitudes and negative images of each other, the researchers' final task was to find conditions that would reduce the intensity of intergroup conflict. As an initial step toward conflict reduction, the groups were brought into contact with each other under conditions that were pleasant but involved no objective competition. These events included things like a common banquet, Fourth of July fireworks, and movies. Instead of reducing conflict, these events simply served as opportunities for mutual namecalling and attack. The common meals, for instance, were marked by shoving and contests over which group would be first in line for food. So much food and paper was thrown around that the meals became known as "garbage wars."

After demonstrating the failure of contact alone to reduce intergroup hostility, the researchers then introduced a new feature into the situation – the presence of *superordinate goals*. The general idea was that if incompatible group goals (i.e. competition) produced hostility, then common goals should reduce it. Superordinate goals were defined as important needs shared by members of both groups that could be met only by mutual cooperation. Common goals were created by facing the Rattlers and Eagles with several urgent situations that required cooperative effort.

One such situation was the breakdown of the water supply system to the camp. The flow of water, which came through pipes from a tank about a mile away, was interrupted and the boys from both groups had to work together to locate the source of the problem. On a second occasion a truck that was needed to fetch food supplies to a camp picnic refused to start and all of the boys had to join in a coordinated effort to pull the truck by rope until it started. Yet a third opportunity arose when members of both groups had a particular movie high on their list of preferences for showing at the camp. They were told that the movie was too expensive to acquire and both groups wound up contributing money in order to rent it.

None of these incidents alone was sufficient to eliminate the strong intergroup hostilities, but the cumulative effect of the series of joint activities did have a significant influence. During the final week of the camp session namecalling and shoving in meal lines had stopped and some friendships were formed across group lines. On the last day, the Rattlers and the Eagles elected to ride home together on the same bus rather than take separate buses (and even stopped along the way for shared refreshments, purchased by one group's remaining prize money).

School desegregation: the record

When one reviews the qualifications of the contact effect, it is clear that many contact situations do not meet all or most of the qualifying conditions. Superficial contacts in formal settings, for instance, or contacts between employers and servants, would not be expected to have any favorable effects on intergroup attitudes; nor would forced contact in situations where local authorities clearly do not support the contact effort. And, indeed, research indicates that contact under these circumstances does little to alter prevailing social stereotypes or intergroup hostility.

Since the historic 1954 Supreme Court ruling, school desegregation in the US has had a controversial history. The original case dealt with legislated segregation, where segregated schools were mandated by law, often requiring that black children be bussed from their own neighborhoods in order to attend segregated black schools at a distance. Since then the courts have also ruled against *de facto* segregation of neighborhood schools, sometimes requiring the development of bussing programs in order to *de*segregate schools within and across districts. As a consequence, the effects of desegregation in school settings have been tested under a great variety of favorable and unfavorable circumstances.

What is the effect of school desegregation on intergroup relations? Reviews of field studies in the US and elsewhere reveal that the answer is "mixed" (Gerard and Miller 1975; Miller and Brewer 1984; Cook 1984; Stephan 1986). Studies in some settings have documented positive racial attitudes under desegregation. The most notable long-term effect is increased likelihood that blacks from desegregated schools will enroll in integrated colleges, live in integrated neighborhoods, and work in integrated employment settings (Braddock 1985). On the other hand, many studies have found that white prejudice against blacks increased following desegregation or showed no improvement. In addition, observational studies have documented the phenomenon of "resegregation," whereby blacks and whites in racially mixed schools rarely interact either because of student preferences in friendship choices (Schofield and Sagar 1977) or because of teaching practices that track or stream children into racially homogeneous groupings (Epstein 1985). Research in both the US and Israel indicates that streaming on the basis of academic abilities seriously undermines the immediate and long-term positive influences of desegregated schooling (Schofield 1979; Schwarzwald and Cohen 1982).

The fact that school desegregation, as practiced, did not have uniformly positive effects on intergroup relations has led some to criticize the validity of the 1953 Social Science Statement (e.g. Gerard 1983). Defenders, however, point out that the statement was directed primarily at the negative effects of legally mandated segregation that existed at the time, and could not have been expected to anticipate all of the forms of mandated desegregation that later developed (Cook 1984). Further, the statement was very careful in specifying the conditions under which desegregation could be expected to be successful. The results of 30 years of field and laboratory experiments on intergroup contact have clearly validated the importance of those qualifying conditions.

Contact experiments: defining the limits

The full version of the contact hypothesis reflected the outcomes of early experience with intergroup contact in natural settings. One aspect of the hypothesis (cooperative interdependence) was systematically tested in the Robbers Cave experiment, and since then many of the other features of the contact hypothesis have been tested in controlled experiments. The results of those experiments have both confirmed and expanded the list of factors that are critical to the effectiveness of contact in promoting positive intergroup relations.

Amount of contact

Most successful integration efforts involve contact over an extended period of time or multiple cooperative interactions. In the Robbers Cave study, a single cooperative incident did not do much to alter intergroup hostility, but several such experiences did make a difference. Some of the first laboratory experiments on interracial contact found that it took intensive interactions between prejudiced whites and a black co-worker over a 20-day period in order to attain significant reductions in prejudicial attitudes toward that co-worker (Cook 1985). Laboratory experiments with artifically created groups have also found that reduction of ingroup bias is a function of the frequency and duration of intergroup interaction (Worchel *et al.* 1977; Wilder and Thompson 1980).

The number of independent contacts with different members of the outgroup also has a significant effect on intergroup perceptions. It takes exposure to many diverse group members to break down stereotypes and the perceived homogeneity of outgroups (Weber and Crocker 1983; Linville *et al.* 1989; Islam and Hewstone 1993). In an experiment with young children, Katz and Zalk (1978) found that exposing white children to multiple black faces reduced prejudice more than face-to-face contact with two specific black children. In general, a variety of contact experiences produces more generalized change than experiences that are limited to a few group members or a single interaction setting.

Intergroup anxiety

In Chapter 3 we discuss the important role that negative affect, such as anxiety, plays in maintaining intergroup prejudice. In recent years, social psychologists have recognized that intergroup contact itself is often an anxiety-provoking experience (Stephan and Stephan 1985; Wilder 1993b). Experiments by Wilder and Shapiro (1989a) provide evidence for a direct link between experienced anxiety and the outcomes of intergroup contact. Anticipated contact with outgroup members in a competitive environment produced intergroup anxiety. When anxiety was high, an encounter with a positive outgroup member did not improve intergroup attitudes. Instead, judgments of the positive outgrouper were assimilated to the negative stereotypes of the outgroup as a whole. When intergroup anxiety was reduced within a cooperative context, however, a positive encounter with an outgroup member did produce more positive evaluations of the outgroup. ·

In a field study of intergroup contact among Hindu and Muslim religious groups in Bangladesh, Islam and Hewstone (1993) confirmed the role of anxiety in mediating the effects of contact on intergroup attitudes. Various measures of the quality of contact between respondents and members of the outgroup proved to be related to reported feelings of anxiety during occasions of interaction. More experiences of voluntary, pleasant, cooperative, and intimate contact with members of the outgroup produced lower levels of anticipated anxiety about future interactions. Lower levels of anxiety were, in turn, predictive of more positive attitudes toward the outgroup as a whole. As with many studies of contact effects, it proves to be the nature and quality of contact experiences, rather than the frequency of contact, that makes the biggest difference in intergroup attitudes. Of particular importance to the quality of interactions is whether or not the contact occurs in a cooperative environment.

Cooperation

Sherif's demonstration that intergroup conflict is reduced in the presence of superordinate goals requiring cooperative effort has been replicated in a wide variety of settings. Blake and Mouton (1986) report experiments involving 150 groups of executives from industrial organizations with results that parallel those of the Robbers Cave study. In each experiment a phase of intergroup competition was followed by a series of cooperative tasks that reduced the negative effects of the earlier competitiveness. Effective cooperation involves at least two important conditions of inter-dependence: shared goals (if one gains, we all gain) and shared effort (we must work together in order to achieve our goals).

Cooperation in the classroom

Probably the most extensive application of Sherif's findings has been the implementation of cooperative learning programs in deseg-regated classrooms. In cooperative learning exercises, children work through lessons or assignments in small groups, teaching each other as they go along. A number of different methods of coop-erative learning strategies have been devised, but all incorporate basic principles of the contact hypothesis (Slavin 1985). One form of cooperative learning is the "jigsaw" technique which was de-veloped by social psychologist Eliot Aronson and has been studied in ethnically mixed elementary school classrooms in Texas and California (Aronson et al. 1978; Aronson and Gonzalez 1988). In the jigsaw method, children are assigned to six-member groups that are academically and ethnically diverse. The material for a particular unit (e.g. a geography lesson) is divided into six parts and each child is given an opportunity to become an "expert" on one section of the unit. In effect, each group member is given one piece of the puzzle. It is then that child's responsibility to "teach" what he or she knows to the other members of the group so that they all can do well on later tests of the material. The idea is to create an environment in which each child has something to gain by learning from each of the others, in a form of positive inter-dependence. This is in stark contrast to the usual competitive atmosphere in classrooms where children score points by perform-ing at the expense of classmates.

Reviews of the effectiveness of implementing cooperative learning strategies such as jigsaw indicate that group learning is associated with increases in liking for classmates, increased cross-ethnic inter-actions, and generalized reduction in ethnic prejudice (Sharan 1980; Johnson and Johnson 1981; Slavin 1985). The success of coop-erative learning methods has been acclaimed as one of the most important contributions of social psychology principles to education. As Slavin (1985: 60) put it, "thirty years after Allport laid out the basic principles, we finally have practical, proven methods for implementing contact theory in the desegregated classroom. These methods are effective for increasing student achievement as well as improving intergroup relations."

Status equality

An important qualification to the effectiveness of cooperative contact as a method of improving intergroup relations is that the conditions promote equal-status interaction among the participants. In many racially and ethnically mixed settings this is not so easily achieved, since participants come into the situation with pre-existing status differences based on group membership. Even if there are no formal status differentials within the cooperative setting, ethnic identity may serve as a generalized cue for expectations of differences in ability and competence. As a consequence, members of higher status groups may be unwilling to learn from or be influenced by members of lower status groups, and their expectations of lesser competence may be reinforced (Cohen 1982, 1984). Under these conditions, the relative positions of members of the cooperative work group are not truly "equal." Cooperation may be undermined when the contributions of the two groups are not well balanced (Garza and Santos 1991).

Cooperative learning strategies attempt to override status expectancies by providing group members with specialized knowledge that makes each member critical to the group's success. But attempts to compensate for initial status disadvantages must strike a delicate balance. We discuss in Chapter 4 how advantaged or high status groups may react to direct threats to ingroup status differences. However, even though status compensation may be regarded as "unfair," it may be a necessary step toward successful intergroup contact, as was demonstrated in an important laboratory experiment by Norvell and Worchel (1981). In the initial phases of this experiment, participants were arbitrarily divided into two groups who then competed on a series of tasks. In one condition, no information was given on who won the competition, but in the other condition, one group was consistently announced as the winner. This manipulation served to establish a "history" of status differential between the two groups.

In the second phase of the experiment, the two groups were brought together to work on a cooperative task. In some cases, one of the groups was provided with a special advantage – extra information that would help in the cooperative endeavor. In other cases, no special information was conveyed to either group. The effect of this special status advantage on intergroup attitudes following cooperation varied depending on the nature of initial group differences. If the groups had previously been equal, the special information created a status imbalance that reduced intergroup attraction compared to the no advantage condition. However, when the two groups were different in status, cooperation did not improve intergroup attraction unless the initially low status group had the special advantage (see Figure 5.1). The special information served to compensate for status inequalities and improved intergroup relations even though the advantage was perceived as "unfair" in all conditions.

The results of this experiment have interesting implications for policies involving affirmative action for disadvantaged groups. Such policies are often regarded as unfair because they violate principles of "procedural justice" (Barnes-Nacoste 1992). But in the long run such policies may improve intergroup relations because they satisfy desires for distributive justice (equal or equitable outcomes for members of all groups) and promote conditions for equal-status contact.

Theoretical perspectives on contact and cooperation

The contact hypothesis and its qualifying conditions were largely derived empirically, from experience with intergroup relations in real-world contexts. Recently, however, more general theoretical perspectives have been brought to bear on understanding the mechanisms through which contact may alter intergroup attitudes and the conditions under which contact will be most effective. Of these theoretical frameworks, the two that have had the most impact are *realistic group conflict theory* (LeVine and Campbell 1972: Chapter 3) and theories of social categorization and social identity.

Realistic group conflict and intergroup relations

Sherif and his colleagues set out to demonstrate a number of points about the nature of intergroup relations in their summer camp experiments. Their work was conducted within the framework of realistic group conflict theory, which holds that the nature of group relations is determined by the actual or perceived relationship between ingroup and outgroup interests. When one group can attain its goals (for resources, status, or power) only at the

Figure 5.1 Effects of inequality on liking for outgroup members

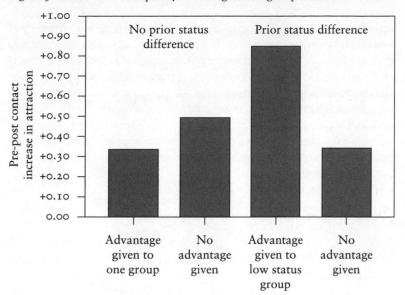

Source: adapted from Norvell and Worchel (1981)

expense of another group, intergroup conflict is the inevitable consequence. Conflict can be reduced only by the acceptance of shared, superordinate goals in place of competing interests.

Most social psychologists accept the idea that competition over scarce economic or social resources heightens intergroup differences and hostility. Experimental studies in the laboratory confirm Sherif's findings, that placing groups in competition increases ingroup bias and discrimination (Brewer 1979) as well as anxiety and negative affect toward the outgroup (Wilder and Shapiro 1989b). In real life, perceived incompatibility of goals is clearly a component of conflict between labor and management in industry, between political groups within nations, and between nations in the global scene (see Chapter 6).

Although objective conflicts of interest certainly play an important role in intergroup relations, some social psychologists argue that competition is not the sole basis for conflict between groups. In some instances, in fact, competition may be the consequence of ingroup–outgroup differentiation rather than its cause (Tajfel 1978; Tajfel and Turner 1986). The minimal intergroup experiments described in Chapter 4 clearly demonstrate that ingroup favoritism and discrimination against outgroup members occurs as soon as individuals are classified into distinct categories, in the absence of pre-existing conflict of interests. According to social identity theory, this happens because positive ingroup identity is attained through comparisons with the outgroup. As Tajfel (1981: 258) put it, "the characteristics of one's group as a whole . . . achieve most of their significance in relation to perceived differences from other groups and the value connotations of these differences." Thus, the need for positive identity creates a kind of "social competition" between groups that is the product (rather than the cause) of ingroup–outgroup categorization.

Social categorization and intergroup contact

Social categorization theory emphasizes the role of cognitive representations of the contact situation as a critical factor determining the outcome of intergroup interactions. When a particular social category distinction is highly salient in a given situation, individuals will respond to the situation in accord with the relevant social identities, acting towards others in the setting in terms of their corresponding group memberships rather than their personal identities (Brewer and Miller 1984; Worchel 1986; Brewer *et al.* 1995). How the interaction is experienced will, in turn, determine the perceptions and attitudes that are expressed during contact and the changes in attitudes that might result from those experiences.

Based on this general idea, three different models of intergroup contact have been developed. These three models are represented schematically in Figure 5.2. Each makes somewhat different predictions of what will be the optimal conditions for effective contact experiences. The rationale and relevant evidence for each of the models will be discussed in turn.

Decategorization: the personalization model
The first model is based on the idea that contact will be most effective if interactions are person-based rather than category-based (Brewer and Miller 1984). A primary consequence of categorization is the depersonalization of members of the outgroup. Social behavior in category-based interactions is characterized by a tendency to treat individual members of the outgroup as undifferentiated representatives of a unified social category, independent

Figure 5.2   Alternative models of cooperative intergroup contact

(a) Decategorization

(b) Recategorization

(c) Subcategorization

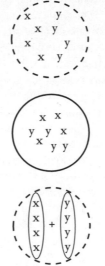

of individual differences that may exist within groups. In situations where visual cues or status differences make participants continually aware of category membership, contact is not likely to break down prior prejudices or stereotypes (Brewer and Miller 1984; Worchel 1986). When category identity is salient, all of the cognitive biases we discuss in other chapters of this text (e.g. Chapters 2 and 4) conspire to preserve and maintain category differences and negative expectations about the outgroup.

Categorization, accompanied by the need for positive distinctiveness (see Chapter 4), leads participants in the contact situation to be selectively attentive to information that differentiates members of the ingroup from members of the outgroup along dimensions that are favorable to the ingroup. Intergroup contact under such conditions should reinforce, rather than reduce, ingroup biases and favoritism. Even if the contact itself is pleasant and free of conflict, it is not likely to have any lasting effects on intergroup attitudes.

This perspective on the contact situation suggests that intergroup interactions should be structured so as to reduce the salience of category distinctions and to promote opportunities to get to know outgroup members as individuals. Attending to the personal characteristics of group members not only provides the opportunity to disconfirm category stereotypes, it also breaks down the monolithic perception of the outgroup as a homogeneous unit (Wilder 1978). The resulting cognitive representation of the contact situation is that depicted in Figure 5.2a. In this scheme, the contact situation encourages attention to information at the individual level that replaces category identity as the most useful basis for classifying participants. Brewer and Miller (1984) assume that such contact experiences effectively break down stereotyping and prejudice because they undermine the availability and usefulness of ingroup–outgroup categorization in interactions with group members.

Evidence for the effectiveness of personalized interactions with outgroup members is provided by results of laboratory experiments with artificially created social categories (Miller *et al.* 1985). In one such experiment, participants first established ingroup identities as "overestimators" or "underestimators" based on their performance in a dot estimation task. Then four-person teams were composed of two members of the overestimator category and two underestimators. The teams engaged in a cooperative problem-solving task in which they had to discuss an issue until they reached consensus on a common solution.

During the cooperative interaction phase of the experiment, some groups were encouraged to be highly task-oriented, to focus their attention on the quality of their solution to the problem. In other groups, participants were encouraged to socialize and get to know each other as individuals. Following the cooperative experience, participants in the task-focused teams still exhibited ingroup bias in their evaluations of ingroup and outgroup members, but those in the more personalized groups showed significantly less ingroup bias (Bettencourt *et al.* 1992).

Personalization of outgroup members can alter intergroup stereotypes, but highly personalized relationships do not always reduce prejudice. Critics of the decategorization model point out that positive interpersonal experiences do not necessarily generalize to attitudes toward the group as a whole (Rothbart and John 1985; Hewstone and Brown 1986). As Wilder (1986b) points out, two elements have to be established for intergroup contact to be considered a success. First, the individual has to establish positive connections to individual members of the outgroup *and* those associations have to be extended to the outgroup category itself.

Experimental studies have demonstrated that positive experiences with a single outgroup member do not readily generalize to the group as a whole unless the individual is viewed as a "typical" category member (Wilder 1984; Desforges *et al.* 1991; Johnston and Hewstone 1992). It is all too easy to define one's friend as an "exception to the rule," and dissociate him or her from the outgroup category (Rothbart and John 1985). As a consequence, personalized interactions may create pleasant contact experiences but do not ultimately change category stereotypes or intergroup prejudice.

Brewer and Miller (1988) acknowledge that highly personalized contact with members of an outgroup may not directly alter outgroup stereotypes. They argue, however, that frequent exposure to the outgroup under personalizing conditions will reduce the salience of category boundaries and increase the complexity and variability of representations of the outgroup as a whole. A review of contact effects by Hamburger (1994) confirms the idea that contact with atypical outgroup members can alter group stereotypes. Experiences with atypical category members may not directly change the central tendency of the group stereotype but it is likely to change the perceived variability within the category. Such changes in complexity and variability of the category stereotype reduce the likelihood of applying the stereotype to individual group members in the future. Ultimately, then, personalized contact can be expected to alter intergroup attitudes in the long run, especially when it involves multiple group members and many occasions of interaction.

Recategorization: the common ingroup identity model

The second model of intergroup contact (Figure 5.2b) is also based on the premiss that ingroup bias is most difficult to overcome when ingroup–outgroup distinctions are highly salient. This model, however, proposes an opposite solution to the reduction of category salience than that represented by the decategorization model. Instead of focusing attention on individuating information in the contact situation, the *common ingroup identity model* (Gaertner *et al.* 1989, 1990, 1993) suggests structuring the contact situation so as to focus attention on superordinate category identification that encompasses both ingroup and outgroup in a single social group representation.

According to the common ingroup identity model, one reason that superordinate goals are effective in reducing intergroup hostility is that they minimize attention to category differences by creating a new inclusive group identity. When such a superordinate category is made salient, group members are more likely to think of themselves as "one unit," rather than two separate groups. Original ingroup–outgroup distinctions become less salient when both groups are included in a new ingroup that encompasses previously separate groups. When this form of recategorization is successful, ingroup loyalties and concern for collective welfare are transferred from the original subgroups to the new social category as a whole.

The model has been tested in a series of experimental studies to assess the conditions under which two previously segregated workgroups can be successfully merged in a superordinate unit. The experimental manipulations in these studies have focused on situational variables that enhance or reduce the perceptual salience of subgroup identities during the combined work-team experience. Symbolic features such as group names and colors, or seating patterns that influence proximity and who interacts with whom, have been varied to control relative salience. Consistently, conditions that enhance the salience of the common team identity and reduce the salience of subcategory identities are found to diminish or eliminate ingroup bias in evaluation of fellow team members. To the extent that participants perceive the combined team as a single entity, rather than an aggregate of two separate groups, evaluations of former outgroup members become more positive. Such a merger of group identities would be represented in organizational settings when two departments are successfully merged into a new functional unit, or when previously segregated male and female workgroups are integrated in a single working unit.

In Gaertner's model, superordinate social identities are created through the merger of subgroups into a single common category that replaces the original category differentiation. An alternative route to superordinate group identity involves making salient an inclusive categorization in which both groups have common membership. Two competing departments, for instance, might be reminded of their common interest in the success of the organization as a whole, or heterogeneous work teams may be created with accountability to the larger organization. This model does not require eliminating subgroup distinctions but relies instead on enhancing the relative salience of common group membership over differentiated categories (Brewer and Schneider 1990).

Subcategorization: the distinct social identity model
A very different approach to promoting effective intergroup contact is that represented in Figure 5.2c. This model is based on the idea

that the need for positive social identity should be capitalized upon in the intergroup contact situation. When intergroup contact experiences are cooperative and pleasant, the effects are more likely to generalize to attitudes toward the outgroup as a whole when contact is experienced as an intergroup interaction rather than an interpersonal one (Hewstone and Brown 1986; van Oudenhoven *et al.* in press). An intergroup orientation is maintained when category identities remain salient in the contact setting.

In order to promote positive intergroup contact, Hewstone and Brown recommend that the contact situation be structured so that members of the respective groups have distinct but complementary roles to contribute toward achieving common goals. In this way, both groups can maintain positive distinctiveness within a cooperative framework. Some evidence in support of this approach comes from the results of an experiment by Deschamps and Brown (1983). Work teams composed of students from two different faculties engaged in a cooperative effort to produce a two-page magazine article. When the representatives of the two groups were assigned separate roles in the team task (one group working on figures and layout, the other working on text), the contact experience had a more positive effect on intergroup attitudes than when the two groups were not provided with distinctive roles.

The subgroup differentiation strategy for effective intergroup contact produces something of a dilemma. On the one hand, if the contact provides positive experiences that disconfirm negative stereotypes about the outgroup, there is reason to expect that attitudes toward the group as a whole will become more positive. On the other hand, such contact also reinforces perceptions that the two groups are distinctly different and thus perpetuates ingroup–outgroup categorization. Associated negative beliefs about the outgroup may also be strengthened, even if the interaction context is a positive one. Thus, the effectiveness of the differentiated social identity strategy depends on the presence of a strong common goal that creates positive interdependence between the groups and overrides other forms of social competition.

Integrating theoretical perspectives

Both experimental and field studies demonstrate that all three models of intergroup contact discussed above can be effective, under

appropriate conditions, in reducing intergroup prejudice and discrimination. Yet there is also reason to believe that all three models
represent unstable solutions to the problems of intergroup conflict
in the long run. Personalized contact may effectively break down
category-based interactions in the contact situation, but category
boundaries may easily be re-established when the context changes.
Both the common ingroup and subgroup differentiation models rely
heavily on the salience of superordinate categorizations and goals,
which may also be highly situation-specific. As contexts change,
the salience of superordinate category membership may diminish
while subgroup identities remain available as a primary basis for
group loyalties and attachment. This is particularly likely when
the superordinate category is a large collective, the psychological
"presence" of which is difficult to maintain.

Unfortunately for all three models, cognitive and motivational
forces conspire to re-establish subgroup differentiation and ingroup–
outgroup distinctions in most social contexts. Brewer's (1991) optimal
distinctiveness theory, discussed in Chapter 2, provides one explanation for why this might be so. This theory postulates that social
identity is driven by two opposing social motives – the need for
inclusion and the need for differentiation. Human beings strive to
belong to groups that transcend their own personal identity, but
at the same time, they need to feel special and distinct from others
(Snyder and Fromkin 1980). In order to satisfy both of these motives
simultaneously, individuals seek inclusion in distinctive social groups
where the boundaries between those who are members of the social
category and those who are excluded can be clearly drawn.

Large, diverse social categories are not likely to have these properties necessary to engage strong social identification and ingroup
loyalties. Within such contexts, individuation fails to meet group
members' need for inclusion and belonging, but inclusion in the
superordinate category fails to meet the need for differentiation
and distinctiveness. Within that context, subgroup identities are
more likely to satisfy members' needs for optimal group identification. In effect, superordinate category identity and awareness of
common goals may be necessary conditions for effective intergroup
contact, but they may not be sufficient to produce enduring changes
in ingroup–outgroup relationships.

One solution to the dilemmas of intergroup contact may lie in
structuring contact situations in ways that contain elements of all
three models. Both common group identity and subgroup identities

may be salient simultaneously, and some degree of individuation may be achieved without denying group identities. This approach relies on extending the cross-categorization effects discussed in Chapter 1 and applying these ideas to the relationship between categories and roles in an intergroup setting.

Within a cooperative group, individuals can be differentiated not only in terms of the different social category identities they represent but also in terms of the different roles or functions they serve in achieving the group's goals. In a sports team, for instance, players take different positions or perform specialized functions. In most work groups, individuals bring different expertise or specializations to the task at hand. In many cases, roles are associated with particular social categories; men are expected to perform different functions than women in the workplace and in the household; and labor and management positions are often divided on the basis of demographic categories.

When roles and category distinctions converge (as in the experimental work teams created by Deschamps and Brown (1983) discussed above), they are essentially redundant. There is no need to individuate the characteristics or contributions of category members because they are functionally equivalent or interchangeable in terms of the roles or contributions they make to the collective effort. As a consequence, the experience of interdependent cooperative interaction within such a work group may ultimately reinforce category distinctions and associated category stereotypes. In contrast to this convergence of category and role would be task structures in which functional roles were systematically (or randomly) crossed with category membership. Under these conditions, the job of getting the task done would require group members to differentiate among members of the respective social categories according to their role or contribution to the team goal. Even if subgroup category identities were highly salient, this categorization would not be sufficient to identify the team member's functional position in the cooperative group. Instead, each individual's contribution would necessarily be separately evaluated in relation to the collective goal.

The comparative effects of convergent and cross-cutting role assignments were tested in a laboratory experiment by Marcus-Newhall and colleagues (1993). The purpose of the experiment was to assess the effectiveness of cross-cutting categories and roles in cooperative work teams for reducing ingroup bias in how the performance and contribution of fellow team members are perceived and evaluated. Members of two artificially created social categories ("overestimators" and "underestimators") were assigned to a four-person work team to complete a problem-solving task. The team consisted of two overestimators and two underestimators, whose category identity was clearly visibly salient throughout the session by the use of colored labels and ID tags.

The team task was structured in such a way that it required the input from two specialized roles or sources of expertise to achieve. The problem given to the teams was to identify the seven most important traits or characteristics that should be used to select potential astronauts for NASA. The job requirements of an astronaut include both technical competencies and social emotional skills. At the initial stages of the team task, individual team members were given one of two scripts to read. Two received a script describing the social-emotional demands placed on an astronaut during a typical space flight, while the other two received a script describing the cognitive and technical demands of being part of a space flight crew. Thus two of the team members acquired expertise in one aspect (social-emotional) of the astronaut job while the others had expertise in the complementary aspects of the job.

Assignment of team members to the respective roles constituted the primary experimental manipulation. For half of the teams, roles and category membership were convergent in that the two overestimators read one script (social or technical) while the two underestimators read the other prior to team discussion. For the remaining half, the scripts were systematically assigned to one overestimator and one underestimator prior to interaction.

Once the differential role assignments had been established, the four members of the team worked together to reach consensus on a single list of seven traits to be submitted as their team product. Teams expected their products to be evaluated against a standard developed by NASA, as a measure of the quality of their performance. (No such evaluation was actually made.) While the results were ostensibly being "scored," team members individually completed a series of questionnaires assessing their ratings of the group experience, evaluations of fellow team members, perceived similarity among members of the team, and trait ratings of overestimators and underestimators in general. The perceived contribution of each team member to the group product was assessed by a reward allocation measure in which each team member distributed "chips" to each of the other team members from a set of chips of up to 100 for each participant.

Of particular interest was the presence of biased evaluations of fellow team members who were members of the subject's own subgroup (ingroup) compared to those who were outgroup members. Indices of ingroup bias on the evaluative and allocation measures were obtained by subtracting mean evaluations (or reward allocations) of ingroup team members from mean evaluations of outgroup members for each individual subject. In addition, the researchers were interested in the effect of team role assignment structure on the perception of differences between ingroup and outgroup members. When ingroup–outgroup differentiation is salient, members of the same group are perceived to be more similar in personality and values than members of different groups. From ratings of interpersonal similarity following team interaction, a similarity index was computed that represented the perceived similarity of team members *across* category identities relative to *within* category similarity.

The direction of results on each of the dependent variables supported the hypothesis that cross-cutting role assignments would result in less intergroup differentiation and less ingroup bias following contact in a cooperative team experience. These effects were particularly pronounced on measures of reward allocation and intergroup differentiation/similarity. In general, the cross-cutting of categories and task assignment succeeded in reducing intergroup discrimination even under conditions where ingroup–outgroup categorization was salient and meaningful.

Assimilation vs. cultural pluralism: is multiculturalism possible?

The three models depicted in Figure 5.2 have parallels in political ideologies and policies represented by different multiethnic nations. Models 5.2a and 5.2b represent variations of assimilationist philosophies, in which ethnic distinctions are submerged in a larger societal identity. Model 5.2c, on the other hand, represents a version of cultural pluralism, in which separate identities are maintained or enhanced.

Much of the debate in the political arena is over the question of whether multicultural societies must choose between assimilationism

Figure 5.3   Alternative forms of ethnic identification in pluralistic
societies

		Value of superordinate culture	
		High	*Low*
Value of subculture	*High*	Integration	Assimilation
	Low	Separatism	Deculturation

Source: adapted from Berry (1984)

or separatism. Proponents of multiculturalism assert that alternative models are possible in which respect for ethnic subgroup distinctiveness and loyalties to a common superordinate group are both achievable. Berry (1984), for instance, has argued that four different forms of ethnic identification are possible in a pluralistic society, depending on how members of distinct ethnic groups relate to their own ethnic identity and to the society at large. Berry's classification system is depicted in Figure 5.3. Integration is the form of intercultural relations in which identification with ethnic subgroups and with the larger society are engaged simultaneously.

Research by Tyler and his colleagues (Huo *et al.* 1994; Tyler 1994) supports Berry's distinction between assimilation, separatism, and integration in how individuals view issues of social justice. Members of ethnic minorities in the US who expressed high social identification with their own ethnic group but not with the superordinate culture defined fairness primarily in terms of *distributive* justice. Fairness for these individuals was judged by the relative outcomes to their own group compared to others. Individuals who scored high on social identification with both their own ethnic group and with the superordinate culture, on the other hand, exhibited more concern with *procedural* justice. They judged fairness in terms of the fairness of the rules and procedures applied to their group, independent of the distribution of outcomes.

The results of experimental studies of intergroup cooperation reviewed above suggest that there are structural arrangements in which the salience of superordinate identities can be achieved without sacrificing identification with distinctive subgroups. Conditions in which subgroups are highly interdependent with complementary roles, or in which roles and category identities are independent, appear to be arrangements that optimize intergroup cooperation. If such arrangements can be generalized to the social policies, they may be critical to multicultural societies.

Some important caveats

The results of social psychological experiments on intergroup contact are promising in suggesting how contact can be structured to optimize the positive effects of cooperative interaction between groups. However, there are a number of reasons why the translation of findings from basic research to application in real-world settings still requires additional research and theory.

For one thing, there is reason to believe that the structural arrangements that lead ultimately to better intergroup relations also elicit initial resistance to team formation and negative attitudes toward the cooperative task. When social identification with subgroup categories is high, the prospect of cooperative interdependence between the ingroup and outgroup raises a threat to group identity (Hewstone and Brown 1986). As a consequence, individual group members approach cooperative settings with (at best) mixed motives. On the one hand there are personal and collective incentives to reach common goals, but there is also a strong reluctance to rely on outgroup contributions to achieve group goals, or to share the benefits of successful achievements with outgroup members. The cross-cutting of role assignments (which reduces the contribution to the team product that can be clearly attributable to the ingroup) may well exacerbate these sources of resistance to cooperative team efforts. Thus, it is extremely important to learn more about the impact of team structure and role relationships on process and performance *across time*. It is very likely that short-term deficits in group functioning may be a necessary price to pay for longer-term effectiveness.

A second potentially important limitation of many social psychology experiments is the lack of attention to status relationships between social groups. The creation of arbitrary social identities in the laboratory setting precludes any history of status differentials between the categories under study. Although the processes of ingroup bias and favoritism may lead members of each group to perceive that their group is better than the outgroup, these biases are symmetric in the absence of any objective status hierarchy. Further, the cooperative structure of laboratory tasks is carefully designed to bring the groups together under equal-status conditions, even when differentiated roles are involved.

In real-world societies, by contrast, intergroup relationships are often played out in the context of well-established status differences among social groups. Further, the nature of the status hierarchy is often such that category identity, functional roles, and position within the society are largely convergent. Such pre-existing status relationships can be expected to moderate the effects of intergroup contact under any structural arrangements and, at a minimum, cannot be ignored within the contact setting (Cohen 1984).

As an initial attempt to address the role of status relationships in a laboratory experiment, Marcus-Newhall (1992) undertook a replication of the earlier experiment on cross-cutting role assignment in the context of a pre-existing status hierarchy. The groups recruited to participate in her experiment were members of college sororities: two that were widely recognized as the highest status groups on campus and two that were among those in the middle ranks of the status system. Preliminary results from this experiment indicate that participation in cooperative teams with cross-cutting role assignment did succeed in reducing status-related biases in intergroup perceptions, whereas cooperative experiences that involved convergent role assignments reinforced ingroup biases on the part of high status group members in particular. Thus, the crossing of category and role contributions to team efforts may prove to be particularly important when status relationships between participating subgroups are asymmetric.

In retrospect, then, the "contact hypothesis" has come a long way since it was discussed by Allport (1954). Experimental and field research indicates that the effectiveness of intergroup contact experiences as a method of reducing intergroup prejudice depends on a complex interaction of the structure and quality of the contact experience, the context in which it takes place, and the frequency and extensiveness of contact relationships. None the less, in the long run, cooperative contact does seem to be the key to improving intergroup relations and changing the social psychological processes that underlie prejudice and discrimination. In the next chapter we turn to the implications of this research for understanding the causes and reduction of large-scale intergroup conflict.

Further reading

Brewer, M. B. and Miller, N. (1984). Beyond the contact hypothesis: Theoretical perspectives on desegregation. In N. Miller and M. Brewer (eds) *Groups in contact: The psychology of desegregation*, pp. 281–302.

New York: Academic Press. A chapter integrating research on the contact hypothesis within the framework of the authors' decategorization model.

Cook, S. W. (1984). The 1954 Social Science statement and school desegregation: A reply to Gerard. *American Psychologist*, 39, 819–32. A review of the outcomes of school desegregation research and implications for social psychological theory.

Gaertner, S. L., Dovidio, J., Anastasio, P., Bachman, B. and Rust, M. (1993). The common ingroup identity model: Recategorization and the reduction of intergroup bias. In W. Stroebe and M. Hewstone (eds) *European review of social psychology*, Vol. 4, pp. 1–26. London: Wiley. A review of the authors' theory of recategorization and related experimental research.

Hewstone, M. and Brown, R. (1986). Contact is not enough: An intergroup perspective on the 'contact hypothesis.' In M. Hewstone and R. Brown (eds) *Contact and conflict in intergroup encounters*, pp. 1–44. Oxford: Basil Blackwell. An introductory overview of research on the contact hypothesis from the perspective of social identity theory.

6 / INTERNATIONAL CONFLICT: WHAT MAKES WAR POSSIBLE?

Much of the content of the previous chapters in this book has been devoted to explaining why intergroup relations are more often characterized by conflict and competition than by cooperative coexistence. Indeed, the psychology of intergroup relations is often equated with the study of conflict and aggression. But when we consider group conflict at the international level, we move from the realm of social psychology into the realms of political science and history. In seeking to explain the causes of war and global conflict, social scientists most often look to political and economic determinants rather than the psychology of individuals. Warfare appears to be driven by institutional forces that transcend individual rationality. Yet, ultimately, wars are entered into, fought, and ended by the decisions and behaviors of individual human beings. Whatever the institutional factors that precipitate and sustain intergroup conflict, it is psychological factors that make war possible in the first place.

The study of the psychological underpinnings of international conflict draws extensively from research on the cognitive and motivational processes underlying ingroup identification, outgroup hostility, and intergroup behavior. Understanding the psychology of warfare provides an opportunity for review and application of basic social psychological research on intergroup relations covered throughout this book.

Theories of human nature: the biological perspective

One approach to the psychology of intergroup conflict attributes the propensity for war to features inherent in "human nature" –

possibly characteristics unique to human beings as a biological species (Goodall 1990). Psychoanalytic and sociobiological explanations for intergroup conflict associate warfare with biological drives of aggression and dominance at the individual level.

"Macho pride:" a motivational basis for war

One of the more interesting psychoanalytic theories of conflict is that proposed by psychiatrist Jerome Frank (1967), who brings together the psychoanalytic concept of "narcissism" at the individual level and national power at the group level. Frank proposes that group power is valued because it compensates for personal feelings of insignificance and helplessness experienced as individuals. By transferring needs for achievement and pride to the group or nation, individuals can achieve a sense of efficacy on a much grander scale than otherwise possible. Ralph White (1984) provides evidence for the operation of such "macho pride" in the history of US-Soviet relations during the cold war era.

A closely related motivational account of intergroup conflict is represented by *social dominance theory* (Sidanius 1993), discussed previously in Chapter 4. Like Frank's theory, the social dominance perspective emphasizes the importance of achieving power and dominance at the level of intergroup (rather than interpersonal) relations. The need for social dominance at the group level is postulated to be an inherent human characteristic that functions to maintain stable status hierarchies in social systems. (It is also of interest to note that Sidanius speculates that the need for social dominance is more characteristic of human males than of the female of the species.)

The genetic imperative

Sociobiological models of human evolution (see Chapter 2) rely on the concept of "inclusive fitness" to account for collective social behavior such as group warfare. In this view, group identity is based on genetic relatedness among members of ethnic groups. The higher proportion of genes that individuals share, the more likely they are to cooperate according to the genetic imperative of kin selection (van den Berghe 1981).

Just as the likelihood of cooperation increases with genetic similarity, the likelihood of conflict increases as the proportion of shared genes among individuals decreases. Ethnic groups evolve to define the boundaries of genetic relatedness, with such groups characterized by ingroup cooperation and outgroup conflict. Like earlier ethologists (e.g. Eibl-Eibesfeldt 1979), many sociobiologists assume that humans are particularly prone to aggressive violence, but directed towards ethnic outgroups (Shaw and Wong 1989). The predisposition to war is an extension of competition for survival between kin groups competing for scarce resources.

Biological theories of group identification and intergroup conflict have received renewed attention in the light of the rise of ethnonationalism in international affairs (Horowitz 1985; Smith 1993; Connor 1994; Gurr 1994). Since the collapse of the Soviet Union and the end of the cold war era in international relations, intergroup conflict seems to have shifted from conflict among nation-states to conflicts over demands for separation and autonomy by ethnic groups throughout the world. A survey in the late 1980s identified 233 politically significant ethnic groups in the world; during 1993–4 these groups were involved in 50 serious ethno-political conflicts or outbreaks of open warfare (Gurr 1994). The apparent virulence of ethnic identification has led some theorists to assume that ethnic identities are primordial – intrinsically more fundamental and stable than other social identities such as superordinate states. Because ethnic groups are characterized not only by shared culture but by beliefs in shared history and common ancestry, they come closest to the extended kinship groups emphasized by sociobiological theory.

The leap from intergroup relations among small ethnic bands to modern international and interethnic warfare is a rather large one, and the basic assumptions of the sociobiological model of intergroup conflict have been criticized on a number of grounds (e.g. Ross 1991). For one thing, the idea that ingroup cooperation characterizes small ethnic bands is not universally supported. In many small-scale societies internal conflict and violence among closely related individuals are very high, even in the absence of resource scarcities (Ross 1986). In the modern international system, both the size and diversity of nation-states and the pattern of alliances in warfare belie the close correspondence between genetic relatedness and war versus peace. Although in recent times the importance of ethnic identification and interethnic conflict would be difficult to deny, most social scientists believe that such identities are socially rather than biologically transmitted.

Perception and misperception: the cognitive perspective

Whereas sociobiologists and psychodynamic theorists place the psychological foundations of warfare in the system of human needs and motivations, political psychologists tend to focus on the cognitive system as the basis for international conflict. In this view, warfare is made possible by cognitive biases and belief systems that limit our capacity for international trust and cooperation. Many of these cognitive biases are rooted in ingroup favoritism and ethnocentric affect discussed at length in previous chapters.

The image of the enemy

The competitive atmosphere that characterizes intergroup relations is a breeding ground for mistrust and misperception. The relationship between competitiveness and social perception was cleverly demonstrated in a laboratory experiment reported by Cooper and Fazio (1986). Participants, who were in groups of three to six individuals, viewed a videotape of a team of two people engaging in a communication task. In one condition, participants believed that they were taking part in a person perception experiment and were instructed merely to observe the dyad. In another condition, participants were told that they themselves would be assigned to pairs who would later compete against the team in the videotape for a cash prize.

During the course of the videotape, the members of the team requested a "time out," which was responded to reluctantly by the experimenter since time outs were not part of the rules of the task. At this point the members of the dyad in the video had a brief discussion and then resumed the task. Thus the nature and purpose of their request for a time out was left ambiguous. After viewing this videotape, participants in the person perception condition tended to interpret the request for time out in a neutral way, assuming it was for the purpose of asking clarifying questions or going to the bathroom. For observers in the future competition condition, however, the request took on more sinister implications.

Most participants in this condition assumed that the purpose was to cheat or gain some unfair advantage in the task. When they evaluated the video team at the end of the experiment, these judges rated them as significantly less honest than did participants in the person perception condition. Apparently, the same ambiguous behavior was deemed to be more suspicious and dishonest when the team on the videotape was a competing outgroup.

Distrust and misattributions of intent are also characteristic of social perception at the international level (White 1970, 1977; Jervis 1976; Silverstein 1989). Nations in conflict tend to perceive each other in remarkably predictable ways. When psychologist Urie Bronfenbrenner returned to the US from a trip to the Soviet Union in 1960 he reported his observations drawn from conversations with Russian citizens (Bronfenbrenner 1961). As he talked with people about US-Soviet relations he found that "the Russian's distorted picture of us was curiously similar to our view of them – a *mirror image*" (p. 46). The view of the enemy's aggressive intent is mirrored in each group's image of the other (see Table 6.1). This image is also characterized by what White (1970) calls the "blacktop illusion," the idea that it is the political leaders of the enemy nation who are evil and aggressive and that the ordinary citizen would actually be in favor of us if they were not deluded and controlled by their leaders.

Although the substance of the "enemy image" has been verified in many contexts of intergroup enmity (Silverstein 1989), as an explanation of the underlying cause of conflict it has an inherent circularity. Some would argue that perceptions of an outgroup as evil and malintended is the product of realistic conflict brought on by competition over scarce resources or ideological disputes. None the less, the readiness with which group members embrace such images of the outgroup is clearly a factor in sustaining intergroup conflict once initiated.

Attributional biases

In previous chapters we have described various forms of ethno-centric biases in the attributions that are made about the causes of ingroup and outgroup behaviors. Such biases are prevalent in the arena of international relations as well. For instance, Burn and Oskamp (1989) reported the results of a 1986 survey of community

Table 6.1 "The Mirror Image:" US and USSR versions

The American view	*The Soviet view*
Russia is a warmonger bent on imposing its system on the rest of the world. Witness Czechoslovakia, Berlin, Hungary, and now Cuba and the Congo. The Soviet Union consistently blocks Western proposals for disarmament by refusing necessary inspection controls.	America is the warmonger bent on imposing its power on the rest of the world. Witness American intervention in 1918 and after World War II with troops and bases on every border of the USSR. America has repeatedly rejected Soviet disarmament proposals while demanding the right to inspect within Soviet territory.
Communists, who form but a small proportion of Russia's population, control the government and exploit the society and its resources in their own interest.	A capitalistic-militaristic clique controls the American government and its media of communication, and exploits the society and its resources.
In spite of the propaganda, the Soviet people are not really behind their government. Most of them would prefer to live under our system of government if they only could.	Unlike their government, the bulk of the American people want peace and disapprove of American aggression. If the American people were allowed to become acquainted with our system of communism, they would choose it as their form of government.
The Soviets do not keep promises and they do not mean what they say. Their talk of peace is but a propaganda maneuver. Soviet demands on such crucial problems as disarmament, Berlin, and unification are completely unrealistic. Disarmament without adequate inspection is meaningless. In pursuit of their irresponsible policies the Soviets do not hesitate to run the risk of war itself.	The Americans do not keep promises and they do not mean what they say. They have no intention of disarming. The American position on such crucial problems as disarmament, East Germany, and China is completely unrealistic. They demand to know our secrets before they disarm. In pursuit of their irresponsible policies the Americans do not hesitate to run the risk of war itself.

Source: Bronfenbrenner (1961: 46–8). Reproduced by permission of the author and the Society for the Psychological Study of Social Issues.

college adults in the US that demonstrated how citizens interpret government actions in ways that preserved positive views of the United States and negative views of the Soviet Union. Causal explanations for similar actions were different depending on whether the action had been initiated by the US or USSR governments. Potentially positive or negative actions by the Soviets (e.g. the 1985 moratorium on underground nuclear testing or the invasion of Afghanistan) were most often attributed to negative causes (e.g. false propaganda, expansionistic motives), whereas ambiguous actions by the US (e.g. invasion of Grenada, bombing of Libya) were attributed to more positive motives or justifications. Also, consistent with the "blacktop illusion" described above, respondents rated the motives and intentions of the Soviet government more negatively than those of the Soviet citizenry.

In a similar series of studies, Sande and colleagues (1989) had American students review newspaper articles describing either benevolent actions (e.g. a whale-saving mission) or negative actions (e.g. arms dealing) attributed either to Americans, Soviets, or French. For US respondents, Soviet actions were interpreted as more self-serving than the same actions by Americans or French, and American actions were seen as most altruistic. Canadian respondents, however, attributed American and Soviet actions to the same motives, suggesting that attributional biases depend on the nature of ingroup–outgroup relations.

The arms race and the psychology of escalating conflict

One problem with the attribution of competitive intent to others is that such expectations tend to be self-fulfilling. When we act to defend ourselves against the expected aggression, our competitive actions confirm the outgroup's expectations of our own intent and elicit competition in return (Kelley and Stahelski 1970). Thus each side behaves in a way that reinforces the other's misperceptions.

Missiles versus factories
Mutual distrust is particularly disastrous in situations involving inherent conflict between motives to cooperate and compete. In Chapter 2 we discuss the "prisoner's dilemma" paradigm as a classic situation in which individual self-interest is served by acting competitively, but everyone's interests are better served by mutual

cooperation. Intergroup behavior is particularly likely to be dominated by competitive choices in such dilemma situations (see Chapter 4).

The arms race between the US and the USSR from 1950–90 has been characterized as a prisoner's dilemma game on a large scale. To study the way people make decisions in such dilemmas, social psychologists have devised experimental games that simulate the arms race in the laboratory (Pilisuk 1984). In one such game, two players each begin with five "missiles." Over the course of five moves, they each have the opportunity to convert any of these missiles into factories (i.e. to disarm). These decisions are made secretly, but at the end of five trials, the payoffs to each of the players are determined by the number of missiles each has at that point, according to the payoff matrix illustrated in Figure 6.1.

The nature of this payoff structure is such that each player is better off if he or she winds up with more missiles than the other

Figure 6.1 The "arms race" game

Number of missiles other person has

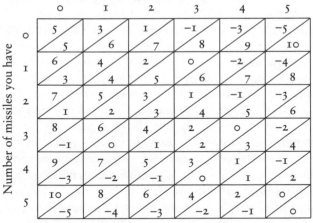

		0	1	2	3	4	5
Number of missiles you have	0	5 / 5	3 / 6	1 / 7	−1 / 8	−3 / 9	−5 / 10
	1	6 / 3	4 / 4	2 / 5	0 / 6	−2 / 7	−4 / 8
	2	7 / 1	5 / 2	3 / 3	1 / 4	−1 / 5	−3 / 6
	3	8 / −1	6 / 0	4 / 1	2 / 2	0 / 3	−2 / 4
	4	9 / −3	7 / −2	5 / −1	3 / 0	1 / 1	−1 / 2
	5	10 / −5	8 / −4	6 / −3	4 / −2	2 / −1	0 / 0

+1 unit for each factory
+2 units for each missile more than other person
−2 units for each missile less than other person

Note: number to left of diagonal is payoff to subject: number to right of diagonal is payoff to other player.

Source: Pilisuk (1984: 299). *Journal of Conflict Resolution*, (28) pp. 296–315, copyright © 1984 by Sage. Reprinted with permission.

player. For instance, if the "other person" ends with two missiles, you are better off if you have three missiles rather than two (even though you also have fewer factories). However, if both players pursue this competitive strategy, they both wind up with nothing (the lower right cell of the matrix), whereas they each could have won five points if they had both disarmed completely (zero missiles each). In studies using this experimental game, Pilisuk found that players wound up with an average of three missiles at the end of the series of five moves. As a result, they both won far fewer points (two points each) than they could have had with a mutual disarmament strategy (five points each). Further, Pilisuk found that if players were given the opportunity to initiate a "surprise attack" after one five-trial sequence, fully one-third of the time at least one player took the attack option even if there was virtually no chance of success from such an attack. Apparently out of fear of the opponent, many players chose a pre-emptive attack rather than risk falling behind in the arms race.

Bases of escalation: vulnerability and deterrence

Choices in intergroup dilemma situations involve risk-taking decisions. In order to achieve mutual benefits, decision makers must determine how much they risk losing if the other players act malevolently, and whether the potential benefits are worth that risk. Kahneman and Tversky's (1979) *prospect theory* provides an interesting account of the psychology behind such risk-taking judgments, with implications for intergroup decision making.

According to prospect theory, the most important factor in risk decisions is whether the decision maker faces the decision in terms of potential losses or potential gains. When individuals make choices between possible positive outcomes, they tend to prefer options that give them a small gain with certainty over more risky (uncertain) higher gains (e.g. most individuals will choose to accept a $100 prize rather than forgo that prize in order to have a ten-percent chance of winning $1,000 instead). On the other hand, when individuals are contemplating possible losses, they are more likely to risk a large potential loss in order to avoid a smaller, certain loss (e.g. if individuals have to choose between giving up $100 versus risking a ten-percent chance of losing $1,000 instead, most choose the risk-taking option).

Applying prospect theory to the realm of international politics, political scientist Robert Jervis (1992) suggests that political decision making is characterized by a "loss aversion" mentality. Conditions of international competition or tension place decision makers in a state of anticipating losses (rather than gains). It is when political leaders believe that they are facing certain loss that they are willing to risk even greater losses in order to have a chance at recovering the *status quo*. According to Jervis, reckless behavior in the international arena is more likely to be undertaken with the aim of recouping losses, or saving a bad situation, than by seeking gains. Situations in which both sides see themselves as operating in the range of losses are particularly dangerous and likely to escalate into war.

The security dilemma

Jervis's analysis of international decision making is supported by results of a series of laboratory experiments conducted by Kramer (1989). In a choice situation similar to that used by Pilisuk (1984), participants had to make a series of decisions regarding investing their available resources in "security" or in a monetary account. Although the security account was worth no monetary value, investment in the monetary account alone left a player vulnerable to a possible "takeover" by other players with a larger security account.

The participants in Kramer's experiments made their investment choices under one of two different decision "frames." For some players, at the beginning of each trial ten resource points were added to their monetary account and they then had to decide how much to leave in that account and how much to move to the security account. For other players, each trial began with the addition of ten points to the security account followed by a decision as to how much to move into the monetary account. From an economics perspective, these two decision frames are equivalent – in either case the individual is deciding how to allocate ten points between two accounts. But the starting point of the decision made a significant difference in the allocations that were actually made. Those who started out with points in the monetary account wound up investing much more into security than those who started each trial with security points. According to Kramer's interpretation, the former players saw themselves as faced with a security deficit and potentially vulnerable to loss of their monetary funds. Players in the other condition saw themselves as having a surfeit in the security account and focused on the potential *gains* associated with investment in the alternative monetary account. As predicted by Jervis, those who were oriented toward loss aversion were more likely to escalate the race for security, thus sacrificing actual gains in the process.

Deterrence beliefs

In addition to perceived vulnerability to loss, investment in preparations for war is fed by beliefs that such preparations will deter other groups from undertaking war. The potentially paradoxical consequences of the deterrence philosophy is well illustrated in this description from Sherif's summer camp experiment (described fully in Chapter 5):

> one group adopted a strategy to deter the other from future raids on its cabin. They collected green apples "just in case," to be prepared. The other group promptly began collecting apples themselves, and these also were hoarded against eventuality of attack. Although expressly forbidden by the research staff and actually prevented on one occasion, the upper crust of one group succeeded in carrying out a raid when both groups had what they considered ample supplies of apples . . .
> (Sherif 1966a: 119)

Whether military build-up does deter war in the international arena is still a matter of much debate among political analysts. But a study by Wallace (1979) suggests that history provides little support for the deterrence notion. Wallace identified 99 serious international disputes in the period between 1816 and 1965. Each dispute involved some movement of troops, withdrawal of diplomatic relations, and other actions bordering on direct conflict. Wallace then classified each incident on two dimensions: (a) whether or not the dispute had been preceded by arms build-up on both sides, and (b) whether or not the dispute erupted into overt warfare. The results indicated a strong association between the presence of an arms race and war. Of those cases characterized by arms build-up, 82 percent of the disputes escalated to war. Without a prior arms race, only four percent of incidents resulted in warfare.

With so little empirical base, why does the belief in deterrence persist so strongly? Ralph White (1984) suggests that part of the reason is that a few specific historic incidents (e.g. Munich and the absence of deterrence of Hitler, the avoidance of nuclear war between the US and the USSR) are particularly vivid and memorable. When policy makers think about deterrence theory, these incidents are most likely to come to mind. Because of the *availability heuristic* (Tversky and Kahneman 1973), the frequency of such events is overestimated (compared to many other historical events that contradict deterrence assumptions) and are overweighted in making judgments.

One particularly interesting form of ethnocentric bias may also be a contributing factor to belief in deterrence. Rothbart and Hallmark (1988) hypothesized that people's judgments about the effectiveness of coercion as a social influence strategy differ depending on whether the target is an ingroup or an outgroup. Participants in their study were given descriptions of a hypothetical conflict situation between two nations, one of which was their "own" country and the other an outgroup. After reading the description, participants were asked to make ratings of the potential effectiveness of various methods for getting one of the countries to reduce the build-up of new weapons. When the intended target was the outgroup nation, various coercive strategies (e.g. threat to build up one's own weapon stocks) were given high effectiveness ratings. But when the ingroup was the target, those same strategies were rated as likely to be ineffective, and more conciliatory strategies were given higher ratings. In other words, people seem to think that "we" will not be influenced by coercion, but "they" will. When both sides of a dispute hold this ethnocentric perception, the possibilities for escalation of conflict are high.

Faulty decision making: the group dynamics perspective

Biological and cognitive perspectives on international conflict emphasize the role of intra-individual processes as factors contributing to war. A more uniquely social psychological perspective places emphasis on factors related to the way in which individuals and groups go about making collective decisions. In Chapter 2 we described research demonstrating the propensity for group discussion to result in polarization of opinions and decisions, and that such polarization is closely related to the formation of strong ingroup identification. We now consider the implications of group polarization for those situations in which groups are making decisions about relations with an outgroup.

The psychology of groupthink

Based on evidence from psychological research and political history, political scientist Ole Holsti (1972) compiled a compelling case for the idea that political decision making under crisis conditions is analogous to individual decision making under stress. Emotional stress and crisis impair rational, realistic thinking in both individuals and groups. Two characteristics typical of crisis situations – time pressure and information overload – are particularly inimical to complex thought and evaluation of alternative options. As a consequence, crisis politics is subject to the dangers of tunnel vision and premature cognitive closure (Lebow 1981).

Following Holsti's analysis, Irving Janis conducted what is probably the most comprehensive review of the forces that interfere with high quality decision making in groups (Janis 1972, 1982, 1989). Janis first became intrigued by this problem when he read historical accounts of the Bay of Pigs fiasco – a major US foreign policy blunder that occurred during John F. Kennedy's presidency. In April, 1961, a small band of Cuban exiles, under the sponsorship of the US, launched an invasion of their homeland at the Bay of Pigs. The plan, developed by the CIA, was to train a squad of commandos and give them the means to launch an amphibious assault on Cuba. The expectation was that once these troops established a beachhead, they would serve as the nucleus for a popular uprising by which the Cuban people would overthrow the Communist regime of Fidel Castro.

As it turned out, events did not unfold as expected. The Cuban military forces easily repelled the invasion, the Cuban people did not rise up against their leader, and the attempt was an embarrassing failure. In retrospect, it was easy to see why the invasion was likely to fail. Why, then, did President Kennedy and his cadre of high-powered advisers not see the major flaws in the plan (e.g. underestimating Castro's popular appeal; thinking that a small band of troops could successfully overcome massive, well-trained armed forces; and so forth)?

Janis studied the details of the group decision processes that led to this, and other government blunders (e.g. Watergate; escalation of the Vietnam War), as well as group decisions on a less grand scale (e.g. those made by airplane crews). From his examination of these situations, Janis developed ideas about a destructive psychological force that he termed *groupthink*.

Figure 6.2 The elements of "groupthink"

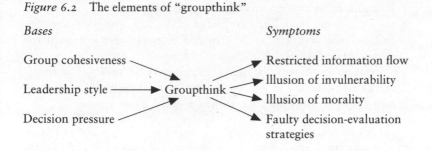

Janis (1972, 1982) concluded that faulty decision making occurs primarily as a consequence of a distorted cognitive style ("groupthink") that prevents group members from evaluating evidence, supporting ideas, and making decisions in a careful, rational manner. In Janis's view, groupthink is generated by specific conditions and is expressed in specific symptoms that are similar to the characteristics of decision making under stress (see Figure 6.2).

Bases of groupthink

Janis identified a number of group dynamics that he thought were the likely determinants of groupthink. He hypothesized that strong *cohesiveness* is one important contributing factor. Cohesiveness involves a sense of camaraderie and the belief that the group is special and worth while. Strong cohesiveness can create an atmosphere in which harmony and good feeling take precedence over critical thinking and expressions of dissent. Similarly, Janis saw the *isolation* of the decision-making group as a potential problem. When a group has limited input from outside sources, the information and options it considers are likely to be incomplete and biased. He also speculated that a closed *leadership style*, in which the leader tends to be autocratic and forceful in presenting her or his preferences, leads to groupthink. Finally, Janis believed that *decision pressure* also contributes to faulty group process. A sense of urgency to come to a decision (partly to leave time for bolstering and rationalizing the choice that is made) minimizes time spent in important orientation and discussion activities.

Symptoms of groupthink

Janis speculated that groupthink is manifested in a variety of symptoms. First, there are a number of factors that operate to restrict the flow of information and ideas among members:

1 pressure from others to maintain the "party line"
2 self-censorship (avoiding expression of deviant opinions) as a consequence of concerns with maintaining a positive image in the minds of fellow group members
3 the presence of mindguards – members who take it on themselves to prevent the intrusion into group discussions of ideas and information that they think would be disruptive.

All three factors limit the information that members have available to consider, with the consequence that a group decision is based on incomplete information and inadequate review of potential options. They also lead members to perceive more unanimity of views than actually exists; thus, the faulty option that becomes the group's choice benefits from support in (illusory) social reality. These are the same forces that operate to produce extremitization of group norms in many settings.

Second, members engaging in groupthink harbor certain illusions about their group, and about relevant outside groups and entities. Group members often believe that their group is highly competent, infallible, powerful, and effective – i.e. they share an illusion of invulnerability. Similarly, they also view their cause as just, guided by the highest ideals, on God's side, and so forth: all expressions of the illusion of morality. In contrast, members can share a perception of relevant outsiders as weak, evil, and easily beaten, thus contributing to the belief that one's own side will prevail. In other words, group discussion tends to exaggerate the components of ethnocentric bias as originally described by Sumner (1906) (see Chapter 2).

Finally, groups whose members are affected by groupthink manifest many signs of faulty decision-making strategies. For instance, groups can become so involved in the details of a plan that they overlook the basic goals they are seeking to accomplish. As a result, a series of smaller decisions are made without consideration of their overall consequences. Bad decisions often escalate, as groups seek to justify their past behavior rather than abandon poor investments (Turner *et al.* 1992).

Research evidence for groupthink

Research conducted to assess the validity of Janis's ideas about the dynamics of small, cohesive decision-making groups has been generally supportive of his perspective. Herek and colleagues (1987), for example, examined a variety of international problems that the US government faced, and analyzed the content of the group deliberations that preceded relevant policy decisions. Results showed that the larger the number of groupthink symptoms observed in the predecision deliberations, the lower the quality of the decisions was judged to be.

Discussion groups studied in the social psychological laboratory have also been found to exhibit symptoms of groupthink, particularly when the groups have high cohesion and share a sense of common social identity (Turner et al. 1992). Cohesive groups sometimes make poor decisions because they are more concerned with protecting a positive image of their group than with the validity of the ideas they are relying on. As we discussed in Chapter 2, social identity is a powerful force for conformity to group norms.

Based on a systematic review of results of groupthink research, McCauley (1989) concluded that Janis may have overestimated the importance of distorted thinking and cognitive biases as the basis of groupthink, and underestimated the importance of compliance in generating flawed collective decisions. Conforming to a group decision does not always mean that the individual agrees with that judgment. Compliance is going along with the group even when one is not personally convinced. Some members might really know better, but do not express their contrary views; instead, they merely acquiesce to the group's choice. Such self-censorship of dissenting opinions appears to be a particularly important ingredient of groupthink. As McCauley suggests, it may not be impaired reasoning but the processes of group decision making itself that produce faulty decisions.

Breaking the cycle of distrust

Although social psychological research sometimes appears to be better at identifying problems that lead to intergroup conflict than at proposing solutions, some social psychologists have taken the additional step of studying how our knowledge of psychological and group processes can be applied to reducing conflict and improving intergroup relations. Irving Janis, for instance, developed a list of prescriptions for leader behavior and group process that would preclude the destructive effects of groupthink (Janis 1982, 1989). These include assigning specific group members the role of "devil's advocate" in the evaluation of each decision alternative, bringing in outside experts to break up the forces of ingroup cohesion, and – perhaps most important – taking time to consider the outgroup's frame of mind and to view the situation from the other's perspective.

In 1962, another social psychologist, Charles Osgood, proposed a potential solution to the problem of the arms race and escalating conflict in what he called Graduated and Reciprocated Initiatives in Tension-reduction (GRIT). The idea behind GRIT is vividly represented in his metaphor of two men on the opposite sides of a seesaw over an abyss:

> John and Ivan stand facing each other near the middle, but on opposite sides, of a long, rigid, neatly balanced seesaw. This seesaw is balanced on a point that juts out over a bottomless abyss. As either of these two husky men takes a step on his side away from the center, the other must quickly compensate with an equal step outward on his side, or the balance will be destroyed . . . both John and Ivan are frightened. Yet neither is willing to admit his own fear because his opponent might take advantage of him.
>
> One reasonable solution immediately presents itself. Let both of them agree to walk slowly and carefully back toward the center of the teetering board in unison. To reach such an agreement they must trust each other. But the whole trouble is that these two husky men do *not* trust other; each believes the other to be irrational enough to destroy them both unless he himself preserves the balance.
>
> But now let us suppose that, during a quiet period in their strife, it occurs to one of these men that perhaps the other is really just as frightened as he himself is. If this were so, he would also welcome some way of escaping from this intolerable situation. So this man decides to gamble a little on his new insight. Loudly he calls out, "I am taking a small step *toward* you when I count to ten!" The other man, rather than risk having the precarious balance upset, also takes a small tentative step forward at the count of ten. Whereupon the first announces another larger step forward as the count is made. Thus John and Ivan gradually work their ways back to safety by a series of self-initiated, but reciprocated, steps . . .
>
> (Osgood 1962: 86–7)

Osgood's GRIT strategy involves unilateral initiatives to reduce tension, which are then escalated if reciprocated by the other side. This proposal draws on knowledge of ethnocentric bias, mutual distrust, and lack of empathy that characterize intergroup perceptions and attempts to put those processes in reverse.

In a real-world demonstration of GRIT, US President John Kennedy announced on June 10, 1963, a unilateral peace initiative halting all atmospheric nuclear testing. The next day in the United Nations, the Soviet Union removed its objection to sending observers to war-torn Yemen, and the United States removed its objection to restoration of full status to the Hungarian delegation to the UN. On June 15, Krushchev reciprocated with an announcement that the production of strategic bombers was halted. In another five days, the Soviet Union agreed in Geneva to the hotline that had been proposed by the United States, and in August, the test-ban treaty was agreed to after having been stalled for a long time (Etzioni 1967).

The GRIT strategy represents one attempt to reverse the psychological processes that lead to the escalation of intergroup conflict and warfare. As this example suggests, understanding the cognitive and motivational mechanisms that make war possible may prove to be the key to prevention.

Beyond the cold war

Osgood's GRIT model and other cognitive theories reviewed in this chapter were formulated during the cold war era of international relations. The basic conceptualization prevailing during that period was that of nations as "rational actors," behaving in accord with their perceptions about the intent and motives of other nation-actors. The demise of the Soviet Union marked the end of the cold war, and with it, changes in perspective on the nature of intergroup conflict. For one thing, the arena of international relations changed from a focus on conflict between two "superpowers" to a multi-group context in which local conflicts and their ramifications predominate. Further, it has become apparent that conflict between groups is as much a product of emotions and symbolic identities as it is of cold cognition (Horowitz 1985; Mercer 1995). In this new climate, social psychological perspectives on ingroup identification and the affective components of intergroup attitudes have become especially relevant.

Concluding perspectives: putting the building blocks together

In many respects, the social psychological study of intergroup relations involves decomposing the phenomena into constituent cognitive and motivational elements. As we said at the outset of this book, understanding the mechanisms underlying prejudice and intergroup conflict engages virtually all areas of social psychological inquiry, including the study of attribution and impression formation, social attitudes, aggression, self-esteem, social comparison, cooperation and competition, and conformity and compliance. These are the "building blocks" of a social psychological theory of intergroup relations discussed in Chapter 1.

But building blocks are just that – components that do not of themselves comprise an integrated theory. From various areas of research we have a wealth of information that is relevant to the understanding of intergroup behavior, but this has yet to be integrated into a single comprehensive model. The study of ingroup bias, stereotyping, interpersonal discrimination, and intergroup contact constitute essentially different lines of research that exist largely in isolation from each other. Certainly, there is justification for studying each of these in its own right. But prejudice is a complex phenomenon that is more than the sum of its parts (Brewer 1994).

An integrated theory will also necessarily take into account the sociopolitical context in which intergroup relations are embedded. In particular, social psychological theories need to be expanded to reflect three important elements of most real-world settings. First, most intergroup relations are embedded in a multigroup context, not just the classic two-category situation that has dominated most research on prejudice and discrimination. Second, most multigroup settings involve some kind of power or dominance hierarchy in which groups differ in access to economic resources, education, and political control. Although social psychological research on intergroup discrimination has looked at the influence of intergroup status differentials (see Chapter 4), the real impact of power differentials has yet to be fully explored. Finally, social psychologists have largely ignored the influence of group leadership on intergroup relations. Research on "groupthink" does acknowledge the influence of leader style on intragroup processes, but this is only one way in which influential leaders or group representatives may play a crucial role in mobilizing ingroup identity and defining the perception of relevant outgroups.

As we discussed in Chapter 1, social psychology is unique in its emphasis on linking structural aspects of groups at the societal level with psychological processes at the individual level. These linkages are yet to be completely mapped, but the cumulative research on ingroup identity, intergroup comparison, and outgroup hostility provides many of the elements of a truly integrated theory of intergroup behavior that now defines the agenda for this crucial area of research.

Further reading

Bronfenbrenner, U. (1961). The mirror image in Soviet-American relations: A social psychologist's report. *Journal of Social Issues*, 17(3), 45–56. Bronfenbrenner's autobiographical analysis of his experience of mutual intergroup perceptions between the US and the Soviet Union during the cold war.

Horowitz, D. (1985). *Ethnic groups in conflict*. Berkeley, CA: University of California Press. An analysis of ethnonationalism and ethnic warfare by a political psychologist.

Janis, I. L. (1972). *Victims of groupthink*. Boston, MA: Houghton Mifflin. The original book describing Janis's model of "groupthink," drawing on illustrations from historical political decisions.

Jervis, R. (1976). *Perception and misperception in international politics*. Princeton, NJ: Princeton University Press. A political scientist's review of the psychology of intergroup images.

White, R. K. (1984). *Fearful warriors: A psychological profile of U.S.-Soviet relations*. New York: Free Press. An application of the "enemy image" perception to US-Soviet relations during the cold war.

REFERENCES

Abrams, D. (1985). Focus of attention in minimal intergroup discrimination. *British Journal of Social Psychology*, **24**, 65–74.

Abrams, D. and Hogg, M. A. (1988). Comments on the motivational status of self-esteem in social identity and intergroup discrimination. *European Journal of Social Psychology*, **18**, 317–34.

Allen, V. L., Wilder, D. A. and Atkinson, M. L. (1983). Multiple group membership and social identity. In T. Sarbin and K. Scheibe (eds) *Studies in social identity*, pp. 92–115. New York: Praeger.

Allport, G. W. (1954). *The nature of prejudice*. Cambridge, MA: Addison-Wesley.

Amir, Y. (1969). Contact hypothesis in ethnic relations. *Psychological Bulletin*, **71**, 319–42.

Ancok, D. and Chertkoff, J. M. (1983). Effects of group membership, relative performance, and self-interest on the division of outcomes. *Journal of Personality and Social Psychology*, **45**, 1256–62.

Archer, J. (1991). Human sociobiology: Basic concepts and limitations. *Journal of Social Issues*, **47**(3), 11–26.

Aronson, E. and Gonzalez, A. (1988). Desegregation, jigsaw, and the Mexican-American experience. In P. Katz and D. Taylor (eds) *Eliminating racism: Profiles in controversy*, pp. 301–14. New York: Plenum.

Aronson, E., Blaney, N., Stephan, C., Sikes, J. and Snapp, M. (1978). *The jigsaw classroom*. Beverly Hills, CA: Sage.

Ashbach, C. and Schermer, V. (eds) (1987). *Object relations, the self, and the group*. London: Routledge and Kegan Paul.

Azzi, A. E. (1992). Procedural justice and the allocation of power in intergroup relations: Studies in the United States and South Africa. *Personality and Social Psychology Bulletin*, **18**, 736–47.

Barnes-Nacoste, R. (1992). About the psychology of affirmative action:

Putting the science back in. Presentation at the annual meeting of the American Psychological Society, San Diego, CA.

Baron, R. A. (1972). Reducing the influence of an aggressive model: The restraining effects of peer censure. *Journal of Experimental Social Psychology*, 8, 266–75.

Baron, R. A. (1979). Effects of victim's pain cues, victim's race, and level of prior instigations upon physical aggression. *Journal of Applied Social Psychology*, 9, 110–14.

Baum, A. and Greenberg, C. (1975). Waiting for a crowd: The behavioral and perceptual effects of anticipated crowding. *Journal of Personality and Social Psychology*, 32, 671–79.

Berg, J. H. and Wright-Buckley, C. (1988). Effects of racial similarity and interviewer intimacy in a peer-counseling analogue. *Journal of Counseling Psychology*, 35, 377–84.

Berkowitz, L., Cochran, S. T. and Embree, M. C. (1981). Physical pain and the goal of the aversively stimulated aggression. *Journal of Personality and Social Psychology*, 40, 687–700.

Berry, J. W. (1984). Cultural relations in plural societies: Alternatives to segregation and their sociopsychological implications. In N. Miller and M. Brewer (eds) *Groups in contact: The psychology of desegregation*, pp. 11–27. New York: Academic Press.

Betancourt, H. and Blair, I. (1992). A cognitive (attribution)-emotion model of violence in conflict situations. *Personality and Social Psychology Bulletin*, 18, 343–50.

Bettencourt, B. A., Brewer, M. B., Croak, M. R. and Miller, N. (1992). Cooperation and reduction of intergroup bias: The role of reward structure and social orientation. *Journal of Experimental Social Psychology*, 28, 301–19.

Biernat, M., Manis, M. and Nelson, T. (1991). Stereotypes and standards of judgment. *Journal of Personality and Social Psychology*, 60, 485–99.

Blake, R. R. and Mouton, J. S. (1986). From theory to practice in interface problem solving. In S. Worchel and W. Austin (eds) *Psychology of intergroup relations*, pp. 67–82. Chicago: Nelson-Hall.

Bodenhausen, G. V. (1993). Emotions, arousal, and stereotypic judgments: A heuristic model of affect and stereotyping. In D. M. Mackie and D. L. Hamilton (eds) *Affect, cognition and stereotyping: Interactive processes in group perception*, pp. 13–37. New York: Academic Press.

Bourhis, R., Giles, H. and Lambert, W. E. (1975). Social consequences of accommodating one's style of speech: A cross-national investigation. *International Journal of the Sociology of Language*, 6, 53–71.

Bourhis, R., Giles, H., Leyens, J. P. and Tajfel, H. (1979). Psycholinguistic distinctiveness: Language divergence in Belgium. In H. Giles and R. St Clair (eds) *Language and social psychology*, pp. 158–85. Oxford: Blackwell.

Bower, G. H. (1981). Mood and memory. *American Psychologist*, 36, 129–48.

Bower, G. H. (1991). Mood congruity of social judgments. In J. P. Forgas (ed.) *Emotion and social judgments*, pp. 31–53. Oxford: Pergamon Press.

Braddock, J. H. (1985). School desegregation and black assimilation. *Journal of Social Issues*, 41(3), 9–22.

Brewer, M. B. (1979). In-group bias in the minimal intergroup situation: A congitive-motivational analysis. *Psychological Bulletin*, 86, 307–24.

Brewer, M. B. (1991). The social self: On being the same and different at the same time. *Personality and Social Psychology Bulletin*, 17, 475–82.

Brewer, M. B. (1994). The social psychology of prejudice: Getting it all together. In M. Zanna and J. Olson (eds) *The psychology of prejudice. The Ontario Symposium*, Vol. 7, pp. 315–29. Hillsdale, NJ: Erlbaum.

Brewer, M. B. (in press). Ingroup favoritism: The subtle side of intergroup discrimination. In D. Messick and A. Tenbrunsel (eds) *Behavioral research and business ethics*. Sage Publications.

Brewer, M. B. and Campbell, D. T. (1976). *Ethnocentrism and intergroup attitudes: East African evidence*. New York: Halstead Press.

Brewer, M. B. and Kramer, R. M. (1986). Choice behavior in social dilemmas: Effects of social identity, group size, and decision framing. *Journal of Personality and Social Psychology*, 50, 543–49.

Brewer, M. B. and Miller, N. (1984). Beyond the contact hypothesis: Theoretical perspectives on desegregation. In N. Miller and M. Brewer (eds) *Groups in contact: The psychology of desegregation*, pp. 281–302. New York: Academic Press.

Brewer, M. B. and Miller, N. (1988). Contact and cooperation: When do they work? In P. Katz and D. Taylor (eds) *Eliminating racism: Profiles in controversy*, pp. 315–26. New York: Plenum Press.

Brewer, M. B. and Schneider, S. (1990). Social identity and social dilemmas: A double-edged sword. In D. Abrams and M. Hogg (eds) *Social identity theory: Constructive and critical advances*, pp. 169–84. London: Harvester Wheatsheaf.

Brewer, M. B., Ho, H-K., Lee, J-Y. and Miller, N. (1987). Social identity and social distance among Hong Kong school children. *Personality and Social Psychology Bulletin*, 13, 156–65.

Brewer, M. B., Manzi, J. and Shaw, J. (1993). In-group identification as a function of depersonalization, distinctiveness, and status. *Psychological Science*, 4, 88–92.

Brewer, M. B., Weber, J. G. and Carini, B. (1995). Person memory in intergroup contexts: Categorization versus individuation. *Journal of Personality and Social Psychology*, 69, 29–40.

Bronfenbrenner, U. (1961). The mirror image in Soviet-American relations: A social psychologist's report. *Journal of Social Issues*, 17(3), 45–56.

Brown, J. D., Collins, R. L. and Schmidt, G. W. (1988). Self-esteem and direct versus indirect forms of self-enhancement. *Journal of Personality and Social Psychology*, 55, 445–53.

Brown, R. J. and Turner, J. C. (1979). The criss-cross categorisation effect in intergroup discrimination. *British Journal of Social and Clinical Psychology*, 18, 371–83.

Brown v. Board of Education of Topeka (1954), 347 U.S. 483.

Bruner, J. S. (1957). On perceptual readiness. *Psychological Review*, 64, 123–52.

Burn, S. M. and Oskamp, S. (1989). Ingroup biases and U.S.-Soviet conflict. *Journal of Social Issues*, 45(2), 73–89.

Burnstein, E. and Worchel, P. (1962). Arbitrariness of frustration and its consequences for aggression in a social situation. *Journal of Personality*, 30, 528–40.

Buss, D. M. (1990). Evolutionary social psychology: Prospects and pitfalls. *Motivation and Emotion*, 14, 265–86.

Buss, D. M. (1991). Evolutionary personality psychology. *Annual Review of Psychology*, 45, 459–91.

Byrne, D. (1971). *The attraction paradigm*. New York: Academic Press.

Byrne, D., Clore, G. and Smeaton, G. (1986). The attraction hypothesis: Do similar attitudes affect anything? *Journal of Personality and Social Psychology*, 51, 1167–70.

Cacioppo, J. and Berntson, G. (1994). Relationships between attitudes and evaluative space: A critical review, with emphasis on the separability of positive and negative substrates. *Psychological Bulletin*, 115, 401–23.

Caddick, B. (1982). Perceived illegitimacy and intergroup relations. In H. Tajfel (ed.) *Social identity and intergroup relations*, pp. 137–54. Cambridge: Cambridge University Press.

Campbell, D. T. (1956). Enhancement of contrast as composite habit. *Journal of Abnormal and Social Psychology*, 53, 350–5.

Campbell, D. T. (1967). Stereotypes and the perception of outgroup differences. *American Psychologist*, 22, 812–29.

Caporael, L. R. and Brewer, M. B. (1991). Reviving evolutionary psychology: Biology meets society. *Journal of Social Issues*, 47(3), 187–95.

Caprara, G. V., Renzi, P., Amolini, P., D'Imperio, G. and Travaglia, G. (1984). The eliciting cue value of aggressive slides reconsidered in a personological perspective: The weapons effect and irritability. *European Journal of Social Psychology*, 14, 313–22.

Carlson, M. and Miller, N. (1988). The differential effects of social and nonsocial negative events on aggressiveness. *Sociology and Social Research*, 72, 155–58.

Cheng, P. and Holyoak, K. (1985). Pragmatic reasoning schemas. *Cognitive Psychology*, 17, 391–416.

Cialdini, R. B. and Richardson, K. D. (1980). Two indirect tactics of image management: Basking and blasting. *Journal of Personality and Social Psychology*, 39, 406–15.

Cialdini, R. B., Borden, R., Thorne, A., Walker, M., Freeman, S. and Sloan, L. (1976). Basking in reflected glory: Three (football) field studies. *Journal of Personality and Social Psychology*, 34, 366–75.

Coates, D. and Winston, T. (1983). Counteracting the deviance of depression: Peer support groups for victims. *Journal of Social Issues*, 39, 169–94.

Cohen, E. G. (1982). Expectation states and interracial interaction in school settings. *Annual Review of Sociology*, 8, 209–35.

Cohen, E. G. (1984). The desegregated school: Problems in status power and interethnic climate. In N. Miller and M. Brewer (eds) *Groups in contact: The psychology of desegregation*, pp. 77–96. New York: Academic Press.

Cole, R. and Bourhis, R. Y. (1990). Power differentials between the sexes: Two intergroup studies. Paper presented at the annual meeting of the Canadian Psychological Association, Ottawa, Ontario.

Connor, W. (1994). *Ethnonationalism: The quest for understanding*. Princeton, NJ: Princeton University Press.

Cook, S. W. (1984). The 1954 Social Science statement and school desegregation: A reply to Gerard. *American Psychologist*, 39, 819–32.

Cook, S. W. (1985). Experimenting on social issues: The case of school desegregation. *American Psychologist*, 40, 452–60.

Cooper, J. and Fazio, R. H. (1986). The formation and persistence of attitudes that support intergroup conflict. In S. Worchel and W. Austin (eds) *Psychology of intergroup relations*, pp. 183–95. Chicago: Nelson-Hall.

Crocker, J. and Luhtanen, R. (1990). Collective self-esteem and ingroup bias. *Journal of Personality and Social Psychology*, 58, 60–7.

Crocker, J. and Major, B. (1989). Social stigma and self-esteem: The self-protective properties of stigma. *Psychological Review*, 96, 608–30.

Crocker, J. and Schwartz, I. (1985). Prejudice and ingroup favoritism in a minimal intergroup situation: Effects of self-esteem. *Personality and Social Psychology Bulletin*, 11, 379–86.

Crocker, J., Thomson, L., McGraw, K. and Ingerman, C. (1987). Downward comparison, prejudice, and evaluations of others: Effects of self-esteem and threat. *Journal of Personality and Social Psychology*, 52, 907–16.

Crocker, J., Voelkl, K., Testa, M. and Major, B. (1991). Social stigma: The affective consequences of attributional ambiguity. *Journal of Personality and Social Psychology*, 60, 218–28.

Crocker, J., Blaine, B. and Luhtanen, R. (1993). Prejudice, intergroup behaviour and self-esteem: Enhancement and protection motives. In M. Hogg and D. Abrams (eds) *Group motivation: Social psychological perspectives*, pp. 52–67. London: Harvester Wheatsheaf.

Crosby, F. (1982). *Relative deprivation and working women*. New York: Oxford University Press.

Crosby, F., Bromley, S. and Saxe, L. (1980). Recent unobtrusive studies of black and white discrimination and prejudice: A literature review. *Psychological Bulletin*, 87, 546–63.

Cross, W. E. (1985). Black identity: Rediscovering the distinction between personal identity and reference group orientation. In M. Spencer, G. Brookins and W. Allen (eds) *Beginnings: The social and affective development of black children*, pp. 155–71. Hillsdale, NJ: Erlbaum.

Darley, J. M. (1966). Fear and social comparison as determinants of conformity behavior. *Journal of Personality and Social Psychology*, 4, 73–8.

Davis, J. A. (1959). A formal interpretation of the theory of relative deprivation. *Sociometry*, 22, 280–96.

Dawes, R. (1989). Statistical criteria for establishing a truly false consensus effect. *Journal of Experimental Social Psychology*, 25, 1–17.

Desforges, D., Lord, C., Ramsey, S., Mason, J., Van Leeuwen, M., West, S. and Lepper, M. (1991). Effects of structured cooperative contact on changing negative attitudes toward stigmatized social groups. *Journal of Personality and Social Psychology*, 60, 531–44.

Deschamps, J. C. and Brown, R. J. (1983). Superordinate goals and intergroup conflict. *British Journal of Social Psychology*, 22, 189–95.

Deschamps, J-C. and Doise, W. (1978). Crossed category memberships in intergroup relations. In H. Tajfel (ed.) *Differentiation between social groups*, pp. 141–58. Cambridge: Cambridge University Press.

Deutsch, M. and Collins, M. E. (1951). *Interracial housing: A psychological evaluation of a social experiment*. Minneapolis, MN: University of Minnesota Press.

Devine, P. G. (1989). Stereotypes and prejudice: Their automatic and controlled components. *Journal of Personality and Social Psychology*, 56, 5–18.

Devine, P. G., Hamilton, D. L. and Ostrom, T. M. (1994). *Social cognition: Impact on social psychology*. New York: Academic Press.

Diehl, M. (1988). Social identity and minimal groups: The effects of interpersonal and intergroup attitudinal similarity on intergroup discrimination. *British Journal of Social Psychology*, 27, 289–300.

Diehl, M. (1989). Justice and discrimination between minimal groups: The limits of equity. *British Journal of Social Psychology*, 28, 227–38.

Diehl, M. (1990). The minimal group paradigm: Theoretical explanations and empirical findings. In W. Stroebe and M. Hewstone (eds) *European Review of Social Psychology*, Vol. 1, pp. 263–92. Chichester, England: John Wiley.

Dijker, A. J. M. (1987). Emotional reaction to ethnic minorities. *European Journal of Social Psychology*, 17, 305–25.

Dijker, A. J. M. (1989). Ethnic attitudes and emotions. In J. P. van

Oudenhoven and T. M. Willemsen (eds) *Ethnic minorities: Social psychology perspectives*, pp. 77–93. Amsterdam: Swets and Zeitlinger.

Dion, K. L. (1973). Cohesiveness as a determinant of ingroup-outgroup bias. *Journal of Personality and Social Psychology*, 28, 163–71.

Dollard, J., Doob, L. W., Miller, N. E., Mowrer, O. H. and Sears, R. R. (1939). *Frustration and aggression*. New Haven, CT: Yale University Press.

Donnerstein, E. and Wilson, D. W. (1976). Effects of noise and perceived control on ongoing and subsequent aggression behavior. *Journal of Personality and Social Psychology*, 34, 774–81.

Donnerstein, M. and Donnerstein, E. (1973). Variables in interracial aggression: Potential ingroup censure. *Journal of Personality and Social Psychology*, 27, 143–50.

Donnerstein, M. and Donnerstein, E. (1975). The effects of attitudinal similarity on interracial aggression. *Journal of Personality*, 43, 485–502.

Donnerstein, M. and Donnerstein, E. (1978). Direct and vicarious censure in the control of interracial aggression. *Journal of Personality*, 48, 162–75.

Donnerstein, M., Donnerstein, E., Simon, S. and Ditrichs, R. (1972). Variables in interracial aggression: Anonymity, expected retaliation, and a riot. *Journal of Personality and Social Psychology*, 22, 236–45.

Dovidio, J. F., Evans, N. and Tyler, R. B. (1986). Racial stereotypes: The contents of their cognitive representations. *Journal of Experimental Social Psychology*, 22, 22–37.

Dovidio, J. F. and Gaertner, S. L. (1986). Prejudice, discrimination, and racism: Historical trends and contemporary approaches. In J. Dovidio and S. Gaertner (eds) *Prejudice, discrimination, and racism*, pp. 1–34. Orlando: Academic Press.

Dutton, D. G. (1973). Reverse discrimination: The relationship of amount of perceived discrimination toward a minority group on the behavior of majority group members. *Canadian Journal of Behavioural Sciences*, 5, 34–45.

Dutton, D. G. and Lake, R. A. (1973). Threat of own prejudice and reverse discrimination in interracial situations. *Journal of Personality and Social Psychology*, 28, 94–100.

Eakins, B. W. and Eakins, R. G. (1978). *Sex differences in human communication*. Boston, MA: Houghton Mifflin.

Easterbrook, J. A. (1959). The effect of emotion on cue utilization and the organization of behavior. *Psychological Review*, 66, 183–201.

Edwards, J. (1985). *Language, society and identity*. Oxford: Blackwell.

Eibl-Eibesfeldt, I. (1979). *The biology of peace and war: Men, animals and aggression*. New York: Viking.

Ellemers, N. (1993). The influence of socio-structural variables on identity management strategies. In W. Stroebe and M. Hewstone (eds)

European review of social psychology, Vol. 4, pp. 27–57. Chichester, England: Wiley.

Ellemers, N., van Knippenberg, A., de Vries, N. and Wilke, H. (1988). Social identification and permeability of group boundaries. *European Journal of Social Psychology*, 18, 497–513.

Ellemers, N., van Knippenberg, A. and Wilke, H. (1990). The influence of permeability of group boundaries and stability of group status on strategies of individual mobility and social change. *British Journal of Social Psychology*, 29, 233–46.

Ellemers, N., Doosje, B., van Knippenberg, A. and Wilke, H. (1992). Status protection in high status minority groups. *European Journal of Social Psychology*, 22, 123–40.

Ellemers, N., Wilke, H. and van Knippenberg, A. (1993). Effects of the legitimacy of low group or individual status on individual and collective identity enhancement strategies. *Journal of Personality and Social Psychology*, 64, 766–78.

Epstein, J. L. (1985). After the bus arrives: Resegregation in desegregated schools. *Journal of Social Issues*, 41(3), 23–43.

Esses, V. M., Haddock, G. and Zanna, M. P. (1993). Values, stereotypes, and emotions as determinants of intergroup attitudes. In D. M. Mackie and D. L. Hamilton (eds) *Affect, cognition, and stereotyping*, pp. 137–66. San Diego, CA: Academic Press.

Esses, V. M., Haddock, G. and Zanna, M. P. (1994). The role of mood in the expression of intergroup stereotypes. In M. Zanna and J. Olson (eds) *The psychology of prejudice: The Ontario Symposium*, Vol. 7, pp. 77–101. Hillsdale, NJ: Erlbaum.

Etzioni, A. (1967). The Kennedy experiment. *The Western Political Quarterly*, 20, 361–80.

Eurich-Fulcer, R. and Schofield, J. W. (1995). Correlated versus uncorrelated social categorizations: The effect on intergroup bias. *Personality and Social Psychology Bulletin*, 21, 149–59.

Feagin, J. R. (1992). The continuing significance of racism: Discrimination against Black students in White colleges. *Journal of Black Studies*, 22, 546–78.

Feinman, S. (1980). Infant responses to race, size, proximity, and movement of strangers. *Infant Behavior and Child Development*, 3, 187–204.

Festinger, L. (1950). Informal social communication. *Psychological Review*, 57, 271–82.

Festinger, L. (1954). A theory of social comparison processes. *Human Relations*, 7, 117–40.

Festinger, L. (1957). *A theory of cognitive dissonance*. Stanford, CA: Stanford University Press.

Forgas, J. P. (1990). Affective influences on individual and group judgments. *European Journal of Social Psychology*, 41, 197–214.

Frank, J. D. (1967). *Sanity and survival: Psychological aspects of war and peace.* New York: Vintage.

Freud, S. (1912/1957). *Totem and Taboo.* In *The Standard Edition of the Complete Psychological Works of Sigmund Freud.* Vol. 13. London: Hogarth Press.

Freud, S. (1921/1960). *Group Psychology and Analysis of the Ego.* New York: Bantam Books.

Gaertner, S. L. and Dovidio, J. F. (1986). The aversive form of racism. In J. F. Dovidio and S. L. Gaertner (eds) *Prejudice, discrimination, and racism*, pp. 61–89. Orlando, FL: Academic Press.

Gaertner, S. L., Mann, J., Murrell, A. and Dovidio, J. (1989). Reducing intergroup bias: The benefits of recategorization. *Journal of Personality and Social Psychology*, **57**, 239–49.

Gaertner, S. L., Mann, J., Dovidio, J., Murrell, A. and Pomare, M. (1990). How does cooperation reduce intergroup bias? *Journal of Personality and Social Psychology*, **59**, 692–704.

Gaertner, S. L., Dovidio, J., Anastasio, P., Bachman, B. and Rust, M. (1993). The common ingroup identity model: Recategorization and the reduction of intergroup bias. In W. Stroebe and M. Hewstone (eds) *European review of social psychology*, Vol. 4, pp. 1–26. London: Wiley.

Garza, R. T. and Santos, S. J. (1991). Ingroup/outgroup balance and interdependent interethnic behavior. *Journal of Experimental Social Psychology*, **27**, 124–37.

Geen, R. G. (1968). Effects of frustration, attack, and prior training in aggressiveness upon aggressive behavior. *Journal of Personality and Social Psychology*, **9**, 316–21.

Geen, R. G. and Berkowitz, L. (1967). Some conditions facilitating the occurrence of aggression after the observation of violence. *Journal of Personality*, **35**, 666–76.

Gelman, S. A. (1988). The development of induction within natural kind and artifact categories. *Cognitive Psychology*, **20**, 65–91.

Gelman, S. A. and Wellman, H. M. (1991). Insides and essence: Early understandings of the non-obvious. *Cognition* **38**, 213–44.

Gerard, H. B. (1983). School desegregation: The social science role. *American Psychologist*, **38**, 869–87.

Gerard, H. B. and Miller, N. (1975). *School desegregation: A long-term study.* New York: Plenum.

Gibbons, F. X. (1985). Social stigma perception: Social comparison among mentally retarded persons. *American Journal of Mental Deficiency*, **90**, 98–106.

Gibbons, F. X., Gerrard, M., Lando, H. and McGovern, P. (1991). Social comparison and smoking cessation: The role of the "typical smoker." *Journal of Experimental Social Psychology*, **27**, 239–58.

Giles, H. (1978). Linguistic differentiation in ethnic groups. In H. Tajfel (ed.) *Differentiation between social groups*, pp. 361–93. London: Academic Press.

Giles, H. and Byrne, J. L. (1982). The intergroup model of second language acquisition. *Journal of Multilingual and Multicultural Development*, 3, 17–40.

Giles, H. and Johnson, P. (1981). The role of language in ethnic group relations. In J. Turner and H. Giles (eds) *Intergroup Behaviour*, pp. 199–243. Oxford: Basil Blackwell.

Giles, H., Bourhis, R. and Taylor, D. M. (1977). Towards a theory of language in ethnic group relations. In H. Giles (ed.) *Language, ethnicity, and inter-group relations*, pp. 307–48. London: Academic Press.

Giles, H. and Smith, P. M. (1979). Accommodation theory: Optimal levels of convergence. In H. Giles and R. St Clair (eds) *Language and social psychology*, pp. 165–77. Oxford: Pergamon Press.

Giles, H., Robinson, W. P. and Smith, P. M. (eds) (1980). *Language: Social psychological perspectives*. Oxford: Pergamon Press.

Goethals, G. R., Messick, D. M. and Allison, S. T. (1991). The uniqueness of bias: Studies of constructive social comparison. In J. Suls and T. A. Wills (eds) *Social comparison: Contemporary theory and research*, pp. 149–76. Hillsdale, NJ: Lawrence Erlbaum Associates.

Goodall, J. (1990). *Through a window: My thirty years with the chimpanzees of Gombe*. Boston, MA: Houghton Mifflin.

Gorenflo, D. W. and Crano, W. D. (1989). Judgmental subjectivity/objectivity and locus of choice in social comparison. *Journal of Personality and Social Psychology*, 57, 605–14.

Gouaux, C. (1971). Induced affective states and interpersonal attraction. *Journal of Personality and Social Psychology*, 20, 37–43.

Greenwald, A. G. (1980). The totalitarian ego: Fabrication and revision of personal history. *American Psychologist*, 35, 603–18.

Griffitt, W. B. (1970). Environmental effects on interpersonal affective behavior: Ambient effective temperature and attraction. *Journal of Personality and Social Psychology*, 15, 240–4.

Guimond, S. and Dubé-Simard, L. (1983). Relative deprivation theory and the Quebec Nationalist Movement: The cognition–emotion distinction and the personal–group deprivation issue. *Journal of Personality and Social Psychology*, 44, 526–35.

Gurin, P. and Townsend, A. (1986). Properties of gender identity and their implications for gender consciousness. *British Journal of Social Psychology*, 25, 139–48.

Gurin, P., Miller, A. and Gurin, G. (1980). Stratum identification and group consciousness. *Social Psychology Quarterly*, 43, 30–47.

Gurr, T. R. (1994). Peoples against states: Ethnopolitical conflict and the changing world system. *International Studies Quarterly*, 38, 347–77.

Hagendoorn, L. (1995). Intergroup biases in multiple group systems: The perception of ethnic hierarchies. In W. Stroebe and M. Hewstone (eds) *European review of social psychology*, Vol. 6, pp. 199–228. London: Wiley.

Hagendoorn, L. and Henke, R. (1991). The effect of multiple category membership on intergroup evaluations in a North Indian context: Class, caste and religion. *British Journal of Social Psychology*, 30, 247–60.

Hamburger, Y. (1994). The contact hypothesis reconsidered: Effects of the atypical outgroup member on the outgroup stereotype. *Basic and Applied Social Psychology*, 15, 339–58.

Hamilton, D. L. and Mackie, D. M. (1993). Cognitive and affective process in intergroup perception: The developing interface. In D. M. Mackie and D. L. Hamilton (eds) *Affect, cognition and stereotyping: Interactive processes in group perception*, pp. 1–12. New York: Academic Press.

Hamilton, D. L. and Trolier, T. (1986). Stereotypes and stereotyping: An overview of the cognitive approach. In J. Dovidio and S. Gaertner (eds) *Prejudice, discrimination and racism*, pp. 127–64. New York: Academic Press.

Hass, R. G., Katz, I., Rizzo, N., Bailey, J. and Eisenstadt, D. (1991). Cross-racial appraisal as related to attitude ambivalence and cognitive complexity. *Personality and Social Psychology Bulletin*, 17, 83–92.

Heider, F. (1944). Social perception and phenomenal causality. *Psychological Review*, 51, 358–74.

Heider, F. (1958). *The psychology of interpersonal relations*. New York: Wiley.

Helson, H. (1964). *Adaptation-level theory: An experimental and systematic approach to behavior*. New York: Harper and Row.

Henley, N. (1977). *Body Politics*. Englewood Cliffs, NJ: Prentice-Hall.

Herek, G., Janis, I. L. and Huth, P. (1987). Decisionmaking during international crises: Is quality of process related to outcome? *Journal of Conflict Resolution*, 31, 203–26.

Hewstone, M. (1990). The "ultimate attribution error"? A review of the literature on intergroup causal attribution. *European Journal of Social Psychology*, 20, 311–35.

Hewstone, M. and Brown, R. (1986). Contact is not enough: An intergroup perspective on the "contact hypothesis." In M. Hewstone and R. Brown (eds) *Contact and conflict in intergroup encounters*, pp. 1–44. Oxford: Basil Blackwell.

Hewstone, M., Hantzi, A. and Johnston, L. (1991). Social categorization and person memory: The pervasiveness of race as an organizing principle. *European Journal of Social Psychology*, 21, 517–28.

Hewstone, M., Islam, M. R. and Judd, C. M. (1993). Models of crossed categorization and intergroup relations. *Journal of Personality and Social Psychology*, 64, 779–93.

Higgins, E. T. and King, G. (1981). Accessibility of social constructs: Information processing consequences of individual and contextual variability. In N. Cantor and J. Kihlstrom (eds) *Personality, cognition, and social interaction*, pp. 69–121. Hillsdale, NJ: Erlbaum.

Hinkle, S. and Brown, R. (1990). Intergroup comparisons and social identity: Some links and lacunae. In D. Abrams and H. Hogg (eds) *Social identity theory: Constructive and critical advances*, pp. 48–70. London: Harvester Wheatsheaf.

Hirschfield, L. (1988). On cognizing social categories: Cognitive development and anthropological wisdom. *Man*, 23, 611–38.

Hirt, E., Zillmann, D., Erickson, G. and Kennedy, C. (1992). Costs and benefits of allegiance: Changes in fans' self-ascribed competencies after team victory versus defeat. *Journal of Personality and Social Psychology*, 63, 724–38.

Hogg, M. A. (1992). *The social psychology of group cohesiveness: From attraction to social identity*. London: Harvester Wheatsheaf.

Hogg, M. A. (1993). Group cohesiveness: A critical review and some new directions. In W. Stroebe and M. Hewstone (eds) *European Review of Social Psychology*, Vol. 4, pp. 85–111. London: John Wiley.

Hogg, M. A. and Abrams, D. (1988). *Social identifications*. London: Routledge.

Hogg, M. A. and Abrams, D. (1990). Social motivation, self-esteem and social identity. In D. Abrams and M. Hogg (eds) *Social identity theory: Constructive and critical advances*, pp. 28–47. London: Harvester Wheatsheaf.

Hogg, M. A. and Abrams, D. (1993). Towards a single-process uncertainty-reduction model of social motivation in groups. In M. Hogg and D. Abrams (eds) *Group motivation: Social psychological perspectives*. London: Harvester Wheatsheaf.

Hogg, M. A. and Hardie, E. A. (1991). Social attraction, personal attraction, and self-categorization: A field study. *Personality and Social Psychology Bulletin*, 17, 175–80.

Hogg, M. A. and Turner, J. C. (1985). Interpersonal attraction, social identification and psychological group formation. *European Journal of Social Psychology*, 15, 51–66.

Hogg, M. A. and Turner, J. C. (1987). Intergroup behaviour, self-stereotyping and the salience of social categories. *British Journal of Social Psychology*, 26, 325–40.

Holsti, O. (1972). *Crisis escalation war*. Montreal: McGill-Queen's University Press.

Holtz, R. and Miller, N. (1985). Assumed similarity in opinion certainty. *Journal of Personality and Social Psychology*, 48, 890–8.

Horowitz, D. (1985). *Ethnic groups in conflict*. Berkeley, CA: University of California Press.

Huddy, L. and Virtanen, S. (1995). Subgroup differentiation and subgroup bias among Latinos as a function of familiarity and positive distinctiveness. *Journal of Personality and Social Psychology*, **68**, 97–108.

Huo, Y., Smith, H., Tyler, T. R. and Lind, E. A. (1994). "Superordinate identification, subgroup identification, and justice concerns: Is separatism the problem; is assimilation the answer?", unpublished ms.

Hymes, D. (1967). Models of the interaction of language and social setting. *Journal of Social Issues*, **23**, 8–28.

Ickes, W. (1984). Compositions in black and white: Determinants of interaction in interracial dyads. *Journal of Personality and Social Psychology*, **7**, 330–41.

Insko, C. A. and Schopler, J. (1987). Categorization, competition and collectivity. In C. Hendrick (ed.) *Group processes*, Vol. 8, pp. 213–51. Beverly Hills, CA: Sage.

Insko, C. A., Pinkley, R., Hoyle, R., Dalton, B., Hong, G., Slim, R., Landry, P., Holton, B., Ruffin, P. and Thibaut, J. (1987). Individual versus group discontinuity: The role of intergroup contact. *Journal of Experimental Social Psychology*, **23**, 250–67.

Insko, C. A., Schopler, J., Hoyle, R., Dardis, G. and Graetz, K. (1990). Individual–group discontinuity as a function of fear and greed. *Journal of Personality and Social Psychology*, **58**, 68–79.

Insko, C. A., Schopler, J., Kennedy, J., Dahl, K., Graetz, K. and Drigotas, S. (1992). Individual–group discontinuity from the differing perspectives of Campbell's realistic group conflict theory and Tajfel and Turner's social identity theory. *Social Psychology Quarterly*, **55**, 272–91.

Isen, A. M. and Daubman, K. A. (1984). The influence of affect on categorization. *Journal of Personality and Social Psychology*, **47**, 1206–17.

Isenberg, D. J. (1986). Group polarization: A critical review and meta-analysis. *Journal of Personality and Social Psychology*, **50**, 1141–51.

Islam, M. R. and Hewstone, M. (1993). Dimensions of contact as predictors of intergroup anxiety, perceived out-group variability, and out-group attitude: An integrative model. *Personality and Social Psychology Bulletin*, **19**, 700–10.

Jackson, L. A., Sullivan, L. A. and Hodge, C. N. (1993). Stereotype effects on attributions, predictions, and evaluations: No two judgments are quite alike. *Journal of Personality and Social Psychology*, **65**, 69–84.

Janis, I. L. (1972). *Victims of groupthink*. Boston, MA: Houghton Mifflin.

Janis, I. L. (1982). *Groupthink: Psychological studies of policy decisions and fiascos*. Boston, MA: Houghton Mifflin.

Janis, I. L. (1989). *Crucial decisions: Leadership in policymaking and crisis management*. New York: Free Press.

Jaynes, G. D. and Williams, R. M., Jr. (1989). *A Common destiny: Blacks and American society*. Washington, DC: National Academy Press.

Jervis, R. (1976). *Perception and misperception in international politics.* Princeton, NJ: Princeton University Press.

Jervis, R. (1992). Political implications of loss aversion. *Political Psychology*, 13, 187–205.

Johnson, D. W. and Johnson, R. T. (1981). Effects of cooperative and individualistic learning experiences on interethnic interaction. *Journal of Educational Psychology*, 73, 444–9.

Johnson, G. R. (1986). Kin selection, socialization, and patriotism: An integrating theory. *Politics and the Life Sciences*, 4, 127–40.

Johnson, G. R. (1989). The role of kin recognition mechanisms in patriotic socialization: Further reflections. *Politics and the Life Sciences*, 8, 62–9.

Johnston, L. and Hewstone, M. (1992). Cognitive models of stereotype change (3): Subtyping and the perceived typicality of disconfirming group members. *Journal of Experimental Social Psychology*, 28, 360–86.

Jones, E. E. (1979). The rocky road from acts to dispositions. *American Psychologist*, 34, 107–17.

Jones, J. M. (1972). *Prejudice and racism.* Reading, MA: Addison-Wesley.

Jussim, L., Coleman, M. and Lerch, L. (1987). The nature of stereotypes: A comparison and integration of three theories. *Journal of Personality and Social Psychology*, 52, 536–46.

Kahneman, D. and Tversky, A. (1979). Prospect theory: An analysis of decision under risk. *Econometrica*, 47, 263–91.

Katz, I. and Hass, R. G. (1988). Racial ambivalence and American value conflict: Correlational and priming studies of dual cognitive structures. *Journal of Personality and Social Psychology*, 55, 893–905.

Katz, P. A. and Zalk, S. R. (1978). Modification of children's racial attitudes. *Developmental Psychology*, 14, 447–61.

Kawakami, K. and Dion, K. (1993). The impact of salient self-identities on relative deprivation and action intentions. *European Journal of Social Psychology*, 23, 525–40.

Kelley, H. H. and Stahelski, A. J. (1970). The social interaction basis of cooperators' and competitors' beliefs about others. *Journal of Personality and Social Psychology*, 16, 66–91.

Kim, H. S. and Baron, R. S. (1988). Exercise and illusory correlation: Does arousal heighten stereotypic processing? *Journal of Experimental Social Psychology*, 24, 366–80.

Klein, M. (1975). *Love, guilt, and reparation and other works: 1921–1945.* New York: Delta.

Konecni, V. J. and Doob, N. (1972). Catharsis through displacement of aggression. *Journal of Personality and Social Psychology*, 23, 379–87.

Kovel, J. (1970). *White racism: A psychohistory.* New York: Pantheon.

Kramer, R. M. (1989). Windows of vulnerability or cognitive illusions?

Cognitive processes and the nuclear arms race. *Journal of Experimental Social Psychology*, 25, 79–100.

Kramer, R. M. and Brewer, M. B. (1984). Effects of group identity on resource utilization in a simulated commons dilemma. *Journal of Personality and Social Psychology*, 46, 1044–57.

Krueger, J. (1992). On the overestimation of between-group differences. In W. Stroebe and M. Hewstone (eds) *European Review of Social Psychology*, Vol. 2, pp. 31–56. New York: John Wiley.

Krueger, J., Rothbart, M. and Sriram, N. (1989). Category learning and change: Differences in sensitivity to information that enhances or reduces intercategory distinctions. *Journal of Personality and Social Psychology*, 56, 866–75.

Larson, R. J. and Diener, E. (1992). Promises and problems with the circumplex model of emotion. In M. Clark (ed.) *Emotion*, Vol. 13, pp. 25–59. Newbury Park, CA: Sage.

Lebow, R. N. (1981). *Between peace and war: The nature of international crisis*. Baltimore, MD: The Johns Hopkins University Press.

Lee, Y. T. and Ottati, V. (1993). Determinants of ingroup and outgroup perceptions of heterogeneity. *Journal of Cross-Cultural Psychology*, 24, 298–318.

Leippe, M. R. and Eisenstadt, D. (1994). Generalization of dissonance reduction: Decreasing prejudice through induced compliance. *Journal of Personality and Social Psychology*, 67, 395–413.

Lemyre, L. and Smith, P. M. (1985). Intergroup discrimination and self-esteem in the minimal group paradigm. *Journal of Personality and Social Psychology*, 29, 660–70.

Lenk, H. (1969). Top performance despite internal conflict: An antithesis to a functional proposition. In J. Loy and G. Kenyon (eds) *Sport, culture and society*, pp. 393–7. New York: Macmillan.

Lerner, M. J. and Grant, P. R. (1990). The influences of commitment to justice and ethnocentrism on children's allocations of pay. *Social Psychology Quarterly*, 53, 229–38.

LeVine, R. A. and Campbell, D. T. (1972). *Ethnocentrism: Theories of conflict, ethnic attitudes and group behavior*. New York: Wiley.

Linville, P. W. (1982). The complexity-extremity effect and age-based stereotyping. *Journal of Personality and Social Psychology*, 42, 193–211.

Linville, P. W. and Jones, E. E. (1980). Polarized appraisals of outgroup members. *Journal of Personality and Social Psychology*, 38, 689–703.

Linville, P. W., Salovey, P. and Fischer, G. W. (1986). Stereotyping and perceived distributions of social characteristics: An application to in-group–out-group perception. In J. Dovidio and S. L. Gaertner (eds) *Prejudice, discrimination, and racism*, pp. 165–208. New York: Academic Press.

Linville, P. W., Fischer, G. W. and Salovey, P. (1989). Perceived distributions of the characteristics of ingroup and outgroup members: Empirical evidence and a computer simulation. *Journal of Personality and Social Psychology*, 57, 165–88.

Luhtanen, R. and Crocker, J. (1991). Self-esteem and intergroup comparisons: Toward a theory of collective self-esteem. In J. Suls and T. Wills (eds) *Social comparison: Contemporary theory and research*, pp. 211–34. Hillsdale, NJ: Erlbaum.

Luhtanen, R. and Crocker, J. (1992). A collective self-esteem scale: Self-evaluation of one's social identity. *Personality and Social Psychology Bulletin*, 18, 302–18.

Mackie, D. M. (1986). Social identification effects in group polarization. *Journal of Personality and Social Psychology*, 50, 720–8.

Mackie, D. M. and Cooper, J. (1984). Attitude polarization: Effects of group membership. *Journal of Personality and Social Psychology*, 46, 575–85.

Mackie, D. M., Hamilton, D. L., Schroth, H. A., Carlisle, C. J., Gersho, B. F., Menesses, L. M., Nedler, B. F. and Reichel, L. D. (1989). The effects of induced mood on expectancy-based illusory correlations. *Journal of Personality and Social Psychology*, 25, 524–44.

MacCrimmon, K. R. and Messick, D. M. (1976). A framework for social motives. *Behavioral Science*, 21, 86–100.

Major, B. (1994). From social inequality to personal entitlement: The role of social comparisons, legitimacy appraisals, and group membership. In M. Zanna (ed.) *Advances in experimental social psychology*, Vol. 26, pp. 293–355. New York: Academic Press.

Marcus-Newhall, A. (1992). "Crosscutting and convergence of category membership with role assignment: Under which intergroup situational features will each lead to reduced bias?", unpublished dissertation. University of Southern California.

Marcus-Newhall, A., Miller, N., Holtz, R. and Brewer, M. B. (1993). Crosscutting category membership with role assignment: A means of reducing intergroup bias. *British Journal of Social Psychology*, 32, 125–46.

Marks, G. (1984). Thinking one's abilities are unique and one's opinions are common. *Personality and Social Psychology Bulletin*, 10, 203–8.

Marks, G. and Miller, N. (1987). Ten years of research on the false-consensus effect: An empirical and theoretical review. *Psychological Bulletin*, 102, 72–90.

Markus, H. and Wurth, E. (1987). The dynamic self-concept: A social-psychological perspective. *Annual Review of Psychology*, 38, 299–337.

McCallum, D., Harring, K., Gilmore, R., Drenan, S., Chase, J., Insko, C. and Thibaut, J. (1985). Competition between groups and between individuals. *Journal of Experimental Social Psychology*, 21, 301–20.

McCauley, C. (1989). The nature of social influence in groupthink: Compliance and internalization. *Journal of Personality and Social Psychology*, 57, 250–60.

McClintock, C. G. (1972). Social motivation: A set of propositions. *Behavioral Science*, **17**, 438–54.

McClintock, C. G. and Liebrand, W. B. G. (1988). Role of interdependence structure, individual value orientation, and another's strategy in social decision making: A transformational analysis. *Journal of Personality and Social Psychology*, **55**, 396–409.

McConahay, J. B. (1986). Modern racism, ambivalence, and the modern racism scale. In J. F. Dovidio and S. L. Gaertner (eds) *Prejudice, discrimination, and racism*, pp. 91–125. Orlando, FL: Academic Press.

McConahay, J. B. and Hough, J. C., Jr. (1976). Symbolic racism. *Journal of Social Issues*, **32**, 23–45.

Medin, D. (1989). Concepts and conceptual structure. *American Psychologist*, **44**, 1469–81.

Meindl, J. and Lerner, M. J. (1984). Exacerbation of extreme responses to an out-group. *Journal of Personality and Social Psychology*, **47**, 71–84.

Mercer, J. (1995). Anarchy and identity. *International Organization*, **49**, 229–52.

Messé, L., Hymes, R. and MacCoun, R. (1986). Group categorization and distributive justice decisions. In H. Bierhoff, R. Cohen and J. Greenberg (eds) *Justice and social relations*, pp. 227–48. New York: Plenum.

Messick, D. M. and Brewer, M. B. (1983). Solving social dilemmas: A review. In L. Wheeler and P. Shaver (eds) *Review of Personality and Social Psychology*, Vol. 4, pp. 11–44. Beverly Hills, CA: Sage.

Messick, D. M. and Mackie, D. (1989). Intergroup relations. *Annual Review of Psychology*, **40**, 45–81.

Messick, D. M., Bloom, S., Boldizar, J. and Samuelson, C. (1985). Why we are fairer than others. *Journal of Experimental Social Psychology*, **21**, 480–500.

Miller, N. and Brewer, M. B. (eds) (1984). *Groups in contact: The psychology of desegregation*. New York: Academic Press.

Miller, N. and Marcus-Newhall, A. (in press). A conceptual analysis of displaced aggression. In R. Ben Ari and Y. Rich (eds) *Understanding and enhancing education for diverse students: An international perspective*. Tel Aviv: Bar Ilan University Press.

Miller, N., Brewer, M. B. and Edwards, K. (1985). Cooperative interaction in desegregated settings: A laboratory analogue. *Journal of Social Issues*, **41**(3), 63–79.

Miller, N., Gross, S. and Holtz, R. (1991). Social projection and attitudinal certainty. In J. Suls and T. A. Wills (eds) *Social comparison: Contemporary theory and research*, pp. 177–210. Hillsdale, NJ: Erlbaum.

Miller, N. E. and Dollard, J. (1941). *Social learning and imitation*. New Haven, CT: Yale University Press.

Mosher, D. L. and Proenza, L. M. (1968). Intensity of attack, displacement, and verbal aggression. *Psychonomic Science*, **12**, 359–60.

Mullen, B. and Hu, L. (1989). Perceptions of ingroup and outgroup variability: A meta-analytic integration. *Basic and Applied Social Psychology*, 10, 233–52.

Mullen, B., Atkins, J. L., Champion, D. S., Edwards, C., Hardy, D., Story, J. E. and Vanderklok, M. (1985). The false consensus effect: A meta-analysis of 115 hypothesis tests. *Journal of Experimental Social Psychology*, 21, 262–83.

Mullen, B., Brown, R. and Smith, C. (1992a). Ingroup bias as a function of salience, relevance, and status: An integration. *European Journal of Social Psychology*, 22, 103–22.

Mullen, B., Dovidio, J. F., Johnson, C. and Copper, C. (1992b). Ingroup–outgroup differences in social projection. *Journal of Experimental Social Psychology*, 28, 422–40.

Mummendey, A. and Schreiber, H. (1983). Better or just different? Positive social identity by discrimination against or by differentiation from outgroups. *European Journal of Social Psychology*, 13, 389–97.

Mummendey, A. and Schreiber, H. (1984). "Different" just means "better": Some obvious and some hidden pathways to in-group favouritism. *British Journal of Social Psychology*, 23, 363–8.

Mummendey, A. and Simon, B. (1989). Better or different? III: The impact of importance of comparison dimension and relative ingroup size upon intergroup discrimination. *British Journal of Social Psychology*, 28, 1–16.

Myers, D. and Lamm, H. (1976). The group polarization phenomenon. *Psychological Bulletin*, 83, 602–27.

Nacoste, R. B. (1990). Sources of stigma: Analyzing the psychology of affirmative action. *Law and Policy*, 12, 175–95.

Newcomb, T. M. (1947). Autistic hostility and social reality. *Human Relations*, 1, 69–86.

Ng, S. H. (1981). Equity theory and the allocation of rewards between groups. *European Journal of Social Psychology*, 11, 439–44.

Ng, S. H. (1982a). Power and intergroup discrimination. In H. Tajfel (ed.) *Social identity and intergroup relations*, pp. 179–206. Cambridge: Cambridge University Press.

Ng, S. H. (1982b). Power and appeasement in intergroup discrimination. *Australian Journal of Psychology*, 34, 37–44.

Ng, S. H. (1984). Equity and social categorization effects on inter-group allocation of rewards. *British Journal of Social Psychology*, 23, 165–72.

Ng, S. H. (1989). Intergroup behaviour and the self. *New Zealand Journal of Psychology*, 18, 1–12.

Ng, S. H. and Wilson, S. (1989). Self-categorization theory and belief polarization among Christian believers and atheists. *British Journal of Social Psychology*, 28, 47–56.

Norvell, N. and Worchel, S. (1981). A re-examination of the relation between equal status contact and intergroup attraction. *Journal of Personality and Social Psychology*, 41, 902–8.

Oakes, P. J. (1987). The salience of social categories. In J. Turner *et al.* *Rediscovering the social group: A self-categorization theory*, pp. 117–41. Oxford: Basil Blackwell.

Oakes, P. J. and Turner, J. C. (1980). Social categorization and intergroup behaviour: Does minimal intergroup discrimination make social identity more positive? *European Journal of Social Psychology*, 10, 295–301.

Oakes, P. J., Turner, J. C. and Haslam, S. A. (1991). Perceiving people as group members: The role of fit in the salience of social categorization. *British Journal of Social Psychology*, 30, 125–44.

Oakes, P. J., Haslam, S. A. and Turner, J. C. (1994). *Stereotyping and social reality*. Oxford: Blackwell.

Orive, R. (1988). Social projection and social comparison of opinions. *Journal of Personality and Social Psychology*, 54, 953–64.

Osgood, C. E. (1962). *An alternative to war or surrender*. Urbana, IL: University of Illinois Press.

Oskamp, S. and Perlman, D. (1965). Factors affecting cooperation in the prisoner's dilemma game. *Journal of Conflict Resolution*, 9, 359–74.

Ostrom, T. M., Carpenter, S. L., Sedikides, C. and Li, F. (1993). Differential processing of ingroup and outgroup information. *Journal of Personality and Social Psychology*, 64, 21–34.

Otten, S., Mummendey, A. and Wenzel, M. (1995). Evaluation of aggressive interactions in interpersonal and intergroup contexts. *Aggressive Behavior*, 21, 205–24.

Park, B. and Judd, C. M. (1990). Measures and models of perceived group variability. *Journal of Personality and Social Psychology*, 59, 173–91.

Park, B., Ryan, C. S. and Judd, C. M. (1992). The role of meaningful subgroups in explaining differences in perceived variability for ingroups and outgroups. *Journal of Personality and Social Psychology*, 63, 553–67.

Perdue, C., Dovidio, J., Gurtman, M. and Tyler, R. (1990). Us and them: Social categorization and the process of intergroup bias. *Journal of Personality and Social Psychology*, 59, 475–86.

Petta, G. and Walker, I. (1992). Relative deprivation and ethnic identity. *British Journal of Social Psychology*, 31, 285–93.

Pettigrew, T. F. (1975). Preface. In T. F. Pettigrew (ed.) *Racial discrimination in the United States*. New York: Harper and Row.

Pettigrew, T. F. (1979). The ultimate attribution error: Extending Allport's cognitive analysis of prejudice. *Personality and Social Psychology Bulletin*, 5, 461–76.

Pettigrew, T. F. and Meertens, R. W. (1995). Subtle and blatant prejudice in Western Europe. *European Journal of Social Psychology*, 25, 57–75.

Pilisuk, M. (1984). Experimenting with the arms race. *Journal of Conflict Resolution*, 28, 296–315.

Platow, M. J., McClintock, C. G. and Liebrand, W. G. (1990). Predicting intergroup fairness and ingroup bias in the minimal group paradigm. *European Journal of Social Psychology*, 20, 221–39.

Prentice, D. A. and Miller, D. T. (1992). The psychology of ingroup attachment. Paper presented at conference on The Self and the Collective, Princeton University.

Prentice, D. A., Miller, D. T. and Lightdale, J. R. (1994). Asymmetries in attachments to groups and to their members: Distinguishing between common-identity and common-bond groups. *Personality and Social Psychology Bulletin*, 20, 484–93.

Rabbie, J. M. and Horwitz, M. (1969). The arousal of ingroup–outgroup bias by a chance win or loss. *Journal of Personality and Social Psychology*, 69, 223–8.

Rabbie, J. M. and Horwitz, M. (1988). Categories versus groups as explanatory concepts in intergroup relations. *European Journal of Social Psychology*, 18, 117–23.

Rabbie, J. M., Schot, J. C. and Visser, L. (1989). Social identity theory: A conceptual and empirical critique from the perspective of a behavioural interaction model. *European Journal of Social Psychology*, 19, 171–202.

Rapoport, A. and Chammah, A. (1965). *Prisoner's dilemma*. Ann Arbor, MI: University of Michigan Press.

Reynolds, V., Falger, V. and Vine, I. (eds) (1987). *The sociobiology of ethnocentrism*. London: Croom Helm.

Richardson, D. R., Hammock, G. S., Smith, S. M., Gardner, W. and Signo, M. (1994). Empathy as a cognitive inhibitor of interpersonal aggression. *Aggressive Behavior*, 20, 275–89.

Rogers, R. W. and Prentice-Dunn, S. (1981). Deindividuation and anger-mediated interracial aggression: Unmasking regressive racism. *Journal of Personality and Social Psychology*, 41, 63–73.

Rosenberg, M. (1979). *Conceiving the self*. New York: Basic Books.

Ross, L. (1977). The intuitive psychologist and his shortcomings: Distortions in the attribution process. In L. Berkowitz (ed.) *Advances in experimental social psychology*, Vol. 10, pp. 173–219. New York: Academic Press.

Ross, M. H. (1986). A cross-cultural theory of political conflict and violence. *Political Psychology*, 7, 427–69.

Ross, M. H. (1991). The role of evolution in ethnocentric conflict and its management. *Journal of Social Issues*, 47(3), 167–85.

Rothbart, M. and Hallmark, W. (1988). Ingroup–outgroup differences in the perceived efficacy of coercion and conciliation in resolving social conflict. *Journal of Personality and Social Psychology*, 55, 248–57.

Rothbart, M. and John, O. P. (1985). Social categorization and behavioral episodes: A cognitive analysis of the effects of intergroup contact. *Journal of Social Issues*, 41(3), 81–104.

Rothbart, M. and Taylor, M. (1992). Category labels and social reality. Do we view social categories as natural kinds? In G. Semin and K. Fiedler (eds) *Language, interaction and social cognition*, pp. 11–36. London: Sage.

Runciman, W. C. (1966). *Relative deprivation and social justice: A study of attitudes to social inequality in twentieth century England*. Berkeley, CA: University of California Press.

Ryan, E., Hewstone, M. and Giles, H. (1984). Language and intergroup attitudes. In J. Eiser (ed.) *Attitudinal judgements*, pp. 135–88. New York: Springer-Verlag.

Sachdev, I. and Bourhis, R. Y. (1985). Social categorization and power differentials in group relations. *European Journal of Social Psychology*, 15, 415–34.

Sachdev, I. and Bourhis, R. Y. (1987). Status differentials and intergroup behaviour. *European Journal of Social Psychology*, 17, 277–92.

Sachdev, I. and Bourhis, R. Y. (1990). Language and social identification. In D. Abrams and M. Hogg (eds) *Social identity theory: Constructive and critical advances*, pp. 101–24. London: Harvester Wheatsheaf.

Sachdev, I. and Bourhis, R. Y. (1991). Power and status differentials in minority and majority group relations. *European Journal of Social Psychology*, 21, 1–24.

Sande, G., Goethals, G., Ferrari, L. and Worth, L. (1989). Value-guided attributions: Maintaining the moral self-image and the diabolical enemy-image. *Journal of Social Issues*, 45(2), 91–118.

Schachter, S. (1959). *The psychology of affiliation*. Stanford, CA: Stanford University Press.

Schofield, J. W. (1979). The impact of positively structured contact on intergroup behavior: Does it last under adverse conditions? *Social Psychology Quarterly*, 42, 280–4.

Schofield, J. W. and Sagar, H. A. (1977). Peer interaction patterns in an integrated middle school. *Sociometry*, 40, 130–8.

Schopler, J. W. and Insko, C. A. (1992). The discontinuity effect in interpersonal and intergroup relations: Generality and mediation. In W. Stroebe and M. Hewstone (eds) *European Review of Social Psychology*, Vol. 3, pp. 121–51. Chichester, England: John Wiley.

Schwarzwald, J. and Cohen, S. (1982). Relationship between academic tracking and the degree of interethnic acceptance. *Journal of Educational Psychology*, 74, 588–97.

Sears, D. O. (1988). Symbolic racism. In P. A. Katz and D. A. Taylor (eds) *Eliminating racism: Profiles in controversy*, pp. 53–84. New York: Plenum Press.

Sears, D. O. and Funk, C. L. (1991). The role of self-interest in social and political attitudes. In M. P. Zanna (ed.) *Advances in Experimental Psychology*, Vol. 24, pp. 2–92. New York: Academic Press.

Sharan, S. (1980). Cooperative learning in small groups: Recent methods and effects on achievement, attitudes, and ethnic relations. *Review of Educational Research*, 50, 241–71.

Shaw, R. P. and Wong, Y. (1989). *The genetic seeds of warfare: Evolution, nationalism and patriotism*. Boston, MA: Unwin and Hyman.

Sherif, M. (1966a). *In common predicament: Social psychology of intergroup conflict and cooperation*. New York: Houghton Mifflin.

Sherif, M. (1966b). *Groups in harmony and tension: An integration of studies on intergroup relations*. New York: Octagon Books.

Sherif, M., Harvey, O. J., White, B. J., Hood, W. R. and Sherif, C. W. (1961). *Intergroup conflict and cooperation: The Robbers Cave experiment*. Norman, OK: University of Oklahoma Book Exchange.

Sidanius, J. (1993). The psychology of group conflict and the dynamics of oppression: A social dominance perspective. In S. Iyengar and W. McGuire (eds) *Explorations in political psychology*, pp. 183–219. Durham, NC: Duke University Press.

Silverstein, B. (1989). Enemy images: The psychology of U.S. attitudes and cognitions regarding the Soviet Union. *American Psychologist*, 44, 903–13.

Simon, B. and Hamilton, D. L. (1994). Social identity and self-stereotyping: The effects of relative group size and group status. *Journal of Personality and Social Psychology*, 66, 699–711.

Slavin, R. E. (1985). Cooperative learning: Applying contact theory in desegregated schools. *Journal of Social Issues*, 41(3), 45–62.

Smith, A. D. (1993). The ethnic sources of nationalism. In M. Brown (ed.) *Ethnic conflict and international security*, pp. 27–42. Princeton, NJ: Princeton University Press.

Smith, E. R. (1993). Social identity and social emotions: Toward new conceptualizations of prejudice. In D. M. Mackie and D. L. Hamilton (eds) *Affect, cognition, and stereotyping*, pp. 297–315. San Diego, CA: Academic Press.

Snyder, C. R. and Fromkin, H. L. (1980). *Uniqueness: The human pursuit of difference*. New York: Plenum Press.

Sorrentino, R. M. and Higgins, E. T. (1986). Motivation and cognition: Warming up to synergism. In R. M. Sorrentino and E. T. Higgins (eds) *Handbook of motivation and cognition: Foundations of social behavior*, pp. 3–20. New York: John Wiley.

Sorrentino, R. M. and Short, J. A. C. (1986). Uncertainty orientation, motivation, and cognition. In R. M. Sorrentino and E. T. Higgins (eds) *Handbook of motivation and cognition: Foundations of social behavior*, pp. 379–403. New York: John Wiley.

Spears, R. and Manstead, A. S. R. (1989). The social context of stereotyping and differentiation. *European Journal of Social Psychology*, **19**, 101–21.

Spears, R. and Manstead, A. S. R. (1990). Consensus estimation in social context. In W. Stroebe and M. Hewstone (eds) *European review of social psychology*, Vol. 1, pp. 81–110. London: Wiley.

Stangor, C. and Ford, T. E. (1992). Accuracy and expectancy-confirming processing orientations and the development of stereotypes and prejudice. In W. Stroebe and M. Hewstone (eds) *European review of social psychology*, Vol. 3, pp. 51–90. London: Wiley.

Stangor, C., Sullivan, L. and Ford, T. E. (1991). Affective and cognitive determinants of prejudice. *Social Cognition*, **9**, 359–80.

Steele, C. M. (1992). Race and the schooling of black Americans. *The Atlantic Monthly*, April, 68–78.

Stephan, C. W. (1992). Intergroup anxiety and intergroup interaction. In J. Lynch, D. Modgil, and S. Modgil (eds) *Cultural diversity and the schools: Prejudice, polemic or progress?* London: Falmer Press.

Stephan, W. G. (1986). The effects of school desegregation: An evaluation 30 years after *Brown*. In M. Saks and L. Saxe (eds) *Advances in applied social psychology*, Vol. 3, pp. 181–206. Hillsdale, NJ: Erlbaum.

Stephan, W. G. and Stephan, C. W. (1985). Intergroup anxiety. *Journal of Social Issues*, **41**(3), 157–75.

Stephan, W. G. and Stephan, C. W. (1993). Cognition and affect in stereotyping: Parallel interactive networks. In D. M. Mackie and D. L. Hamilton (eds) *Affect, cognition, and stereotyping*, pp. 111–36. San Diego, CA: Academic Press.

Stouffer, S., Suchman, E., DeVinney, L., Stat, S. and Williams, R. (1949). *The American soldier: Adjustments during army life*, Vol. 1. Princeton, NJ: Princeton University Press.

Stroessner, S. J. and Mackie, D. M. (1993). Affect and perceived group variability: Implications for stereotyping and prejudice. In D. M. Mackie and D. L. Hamilton (eds) *Affect, cognition, and stereotyping*, pp. 63–86. San Diego, CA: Academic Press.

Struch, N. and Schwartz, S. H. (1989). Intergroup aggression: Its predictors and distinctness from in-group bias. *Journal of Personality and Social Psychology*, **56**, 364–73.

Sumner, W. G. (1906). *Folkways*. New York: Ginn.

Swann, W. B. (1987). Identity negotiation: Where two roads meet. *Journal of Personality and Social Psychology*, **53**, 1038–51.

Tajfel, H. (1969). Cognitive aspects of prejudice. *Journal of Social Issues*, **25**, 79–97.

Tajfel, H. (1970). Experiments in intergroup discrimination. *Scientific American*, **223**(2), 96–102.

Tajfel, H. (1978). *Differentiation between social groups: Studies in the social psychology of intergroup relations*. London: Academic Press.

Tajfel, H. (1979). Individuals and groups in social psychology. *British Journal of Social and Clinical Psychology*, **18**, 183–90.

Tajfel, H. (1981). *Human groups and social categories*. Cambridge: Cambridge University Press.

Tajfel, H. and Forgas, J. P. (1981). Social categorization: Cognitions, values and groups. In J. Forgas (ed.) *Social cognition*, pp. 111–40. London: Academic Press.

Tajfel, H. and Turner, J. C. (1986). The social identity theory of intergroup behavior. In S. Worchel and W. Austin (eds) *Psychology of intergroup relations*, pp. 7–24. Chicago: Nelson-Hall.

Tajfel, H. and Wilkes, A. (1963). Classification and quantitative judgement. *British Journal of Psychology*, **54**, 101–13.

Tajfel, H., Nemeth, C., Jahoda, G., Campbell, J. and Johnson, N. (1970). The development of children's preference for their own country: A cross-national study. *International Journal of Psychology*, **5**, 245–53.

Tajfel, H., Billig, M., Bundy, R. and Flament, C. (1971). Social categorization and intergroup behaviour. *European Journal of Social Psychology*, **1**, 149–78.

Taylor, D. M. and McKirnan, D. J. (1984). A five-stage model of intergroup relations. *British Journal of Social Psychology*, **23**, 291–300.

Taylor, D. M. and Moghaddam, F. M. (1994). *Theories of intergroup relations: international social psychological perspectives*. London: Praeger.

Taylor, D. M., Moghaddam, F. M., Gamble, I. and Zellerer, E. (1987). Disadvantaged group responses to perceived inequality: From passive acceptance to collective action. *Journal of Social Psychology*, **127**, 259–72.

Taylor, D. M., Wright, S., Moghaddam, F. and Lalonde, R. (1990). The personal/group discrimination discrepancy: Perceiving my group but not myself to be a target for discrimination. *Personality and Social Psychology Bulletin*, **16**, 254–62.

Taylor, S. E. and Brown, J. D. (1988). Illusion and well-being: A social psychological perspective on mental health. *Psychological Bulletin*, **103**, 193–210.

Trafimow, D., Triandis, H. C. and Goto, S. G. (1991). Some tests of the distinction between the private self and the collective self. *Journal of Personality and Social Psychology*, **60**, 649–55.

Triandis, H. C. (1989). The self and social behavior in differing cultural contexts. *Psychological Review*, **96**, 506–20.

Turner, J. C. (1975). Social comparison and social identity: Some prospects for intergroup behaviour. *European Journal of Social Psychology*, **5**, 5–34.

Turner, J. C. (1978). Social categorization and social discrimination in the minimal group paradigm. In H. Tajfel (ed.) *Differentiation between social groups*, pp. 101–40. London: Academic Press.

Turner, J. C. (1981). The experimental social psychology of intergroup behaviour. In J. Turner and H. Giles (eds) *Intergroup behaviour*,
pp. 66–101. Oxford: Blackwell.

Turner, J. C. (1982). Towards a cognitive redefinition of the social group.
In H. Tajfel (ed.) *Social identity and intergroup relations*, pp. 15–40.
Cambridge: Cambridge University Press.

Turner, J. C. (1984). Social identification and psychological group
formation. In H. Tajfel (ed.) *The social dimension: European
developments in social psychology*, Vol. 2, pp. 518–40. Cambridge:
Cambridge University Press.

Turner, J. C. (1985). Social categorization and the self-concept: A social
cognitive theory of group behavior. In E. Lawler (ed.) *Advances in
group processes*, Vol. 2, pp. 77–122. Greenwich, CN: JAI Press.

Turner, J. C. (1991). *Social influence*. Buckingham: Open University
Press.

Turner, J. C. and Brown, R. (1978). Social status, cognitive alternatives
and intergroup relations. In H. Tajfel (ed.) *Differentiation between
social groups*, pp. 201–34. London: Academic Press.

Turner, J. C., Hogg, M., Turner, P. and Smith, P. (1984). Failure and defeat
as determinants of group cohesiveness. *British Journal of Social
Psychology*, 23, 97–111.

Turner, J. C., Hogg, M., Oakes, P., Reicher, S. and Wetherell, M. (1987).
Rediscovering the social group: A self-categorization theory. Oxford:
Basil Blackwell.

Turner, J. C., Wetherell, M. S. and Hogg, M. A. (1989). Referent
informational influence and group polarization. *British Journal of
Social Psychology*, 28, 135–47.

Turner, M., Pratkanis, A., Probasco, P. and Leve, C. (1992). Threat,
cohesion, and group effectiveness: Testing a social identity maintenance perspective on groupthink. *Journal of Personality and Social
Psychology*, 63, 781–96.

Tversky, A. and Kahneman, D. (1973). Availability: A heuristic for
judging frequency and probability. *Cognitive Psychology*, 5, 207–32.

Tyler, T. R. (1994). Psychological models of the justice motive: The
antecedents of distributive justice and procedural justice. *Journal of
Personality and Social Psychology*, 67, 850–63.

Vanbeselaere, N. (1987). The effects of dichotomous and crossed social
categorizations upon intergroup discrimination. *European Journal of
Social Psychology*, 17, 143–56.

van den Berghe, P. L. (1981). *The Ethnic Phenomenon*. New York: Elsevier.

van Knippenberg, A. and Ellemers, N. (1990). Social identity and intergroup differentiation processes. In W. Stroebe and M. Hewstone
(eds) *European review of social psychology*, Vol. 1, pp. 137–69.
Chichester, England: John Wiley.

van Knippenberg, A. and Ellemers, N. (1993). Strategies in intergroup relations. In M. Hogg and D. Abrams (eds) *Group motivation: Social psychological perspectives*, pp. 17–32. London: Harvester Wheatsheaf.

van Knippenberg, A. and van Oers, H. (1984). Social identity and equity concerns in intergroup perceptions. *British Journal of Social Psychology*, 23, 351–61.

van Knippenberg, A., van Twuyver, M. and Pepels, J. (1994). Factors affecting social categorization processes in memory. *British Journal of Social Psychology*, 33, 419–31.

Vanneman, R. D. and Pettigrew, T. F. (1972). Race and relative deprivation in the urban United States. *Race*, 13, 461–86.

van Oudenhoven, J. P., Groenewoud, J. T. and Hewstone, M. (in press). Cooperation, ethnic salience and generalization of interethnic attitudes. *European Journal of Social Psychology*.

Volkan, V. D. (1988). *The need to have enemies and allies*. Northvale, NJ: Jason Aronson.

Wagner, U. and Ward, P. I. (1993). Variation of out-group presence and evaluation of the in-group. *British Journal of Social Psychology*, 32, 241–51.

Walker, I. and Pettigrew, T. F. (1984). Relative deprivation theory: An overview and conceptual critique. *British Journal of Social Psychology*, 23, 301–10.

Wallace, M. D. (1979). Arms races and escalation: Some new evidence. In J. Singer (ed.) *Explaining war: Selected papers from the correlates of war project*, pp. 54–70. Beverly Hills, CA: Sage.

Walster, E., Walster, G. and Berscheid, E. (1978). *Equity: Theory and research*. Boston, MA: Allyn and Bacon.

Weber, J. G. (1994). The nature of ethnocentric attribution bias: Ingroup protection or enhancement? *Journal of Experimental Social Psychology*, 30, 482–504.

Weber, R. and Crocker, J. C. (1983). Cognitive processes in the revision of stereotypic beliefs. *Journal of Personality and Social Psychology*, 45, 961–7.

Wegener, D. T. and Petty, R. E. (1994). Mood management across affective states: The hedonic contingency hypothesis. *Journal of Personality and Social Psychology*, 66, 1034–48.

Weiner, B. (1985). An attributional theory of motivation and emotion. *Psychological Review*, 92, 548–73.

Weiner, B. (1986). *An attributional theory of motivation and emotion*. New York: Springer-Verlag.

Weiner, B., Amirkhan, J., Folkes, V. and Verette, J. (1987). An attributional analysis of excuse giving: Studies of a naive theory of emotion. *Journal of Personality and Social Psychology*, 52, 316–24.

Wetherell, M. S. (1987). Social identity and group polarization. In J. Turner et al. *Rediscovering the social group: A self-categorization theory*, pp. 142–70. Oxford: Basil Blackwell.

White, R. K. (1970). *Nobody wanted war: Misperceptions in Vietnam and other wars*. Garden City, NY: Doubleday.

White, R. K. (1977). Misperception in the Arab-Israeli conflict. *Journal of Social Issues*, 33(1), 190–221.

White, R. K. (1984). *Fearful warriors: A psychological profile of U.S.-Soviet relations*. New York: Free Press.

Wilder, D. A. (1978). Reduction of intergroup discrimination through individuation of the outgroup. *Journal of Personality and Social Psychology*, 36, 1361–74.

Wilder, D. A. (1981). Perceiving persons as a group: Categorization and intergroup relations. In D. Hamilton (ed.) *Cognitive processes in stereotyping and intergroup behavior*, pp. 213–57. Hillsdale, NJ: Erlbaum.

Wilder, D. A. (1984). Intergroup contact: The typical member and the exception to the rule. *Journal of Experimental Social Psychology*, 20, 177–94.

Wilder, D. A. (1986a). Social categorization: Implications for creation and reduction of intergroup bias. In L. Berkowitz (ed.) *Advances in experimental social psychology*, Vol. 19, pp. 291–355. New York: Academic Press.

Wilder, D. A. (1986b). Cognitive factors affecting the success of intergroup contact. In S. Worchel and W. Austin (eds) *Psychology of intergroup relations*, pp. 49–66. Chicago: Nelson-Hall.

Wilder, D. A. (1993a). Freezing intergroup evaluations: Anxiety fosters resistance to counterstereotypic information. In M. S. Hogg and D. Abrams (eds) *Group motivation: Social psychological perspectives*, pp. 68–86. New York: Harvester Wheatsheaf.

Wilder, D. A. (1993b). The role of anxiety in facilitating stereotypic judgment of outgroup behavior. In D. M. Mackie and D. L. Hamilton (eds) *Affect, cognition, and stereotyping*, pp. 87–109. San Diego, CA: Academic Press.

Wilder, D. A. and Shapiro, P. N. (1984). Role of outgroup cues in determining social identity. *Journal of Personality and Social Psychology*, 47, 342–8.

Wilder, D. A. and Shapiro, P. N. (1989a). Role of competition-induced anxiety in limiting the beneficial impact of positive behavior by an out-group member. *Journal of Personality and Social Psychology*, 56, 60–9.

Wilder, D. A. and Shapiro, P. N. (1989b). Effects of anxiety on impression formation in a group context: An anxiety-assimilation hypothesis. *Journal of Experimental Social Psychology*, 25, 481–99.

Wilder, D. A. and Thompson, J. E. (1980). Intergroup contact with independent manipulations of in-group and out-group interaction. *Journal of Personality and Social Psychology*, 38, 589–603.

Wills, T. A. (1981). Downward comparison principles in social psychology. *Psychological Bulletin*, 90, 249–63.

Wilson, L. and Rogers, R. W. (1975). The fire this time: Effects of race of target, insult, and potential retaliation on black aggression. *Journal of Personality and Social Psychology*, 32, 857–64.

Wilson, W. and Kayatani, M. (1968). Intergroup attitudes and strategies in games between opponents of the same or of a different race. *Journal of Personality and Social Psychology*, 9, 24–30.

Worchel, S. (1986). The role of cooperation in reducing intergroup conflict. In S. Worchel and W. Austin (eds) *Psychology of intergroup relations*, pp. 288–304. Chicago: Nelson-Hall.

Worchel, S., Andreoli, V. and Folger, R. (1977). Intergroup cooperation and intergroup attraction: The effect of previous interaction and outcome of combined effort. *Journal of Experimental Social Psychology*, 13, 131–40.

Wright, S. C., Taylor, D. M. and Moghaddam, F. M. (1990). Responding to membership in a disadvantaged group: From acceptance to collective protest. *Journal of Personality and Social Psychology*, 58, 994–1003.

Zanna, M., Crosby, F. and Loewenstein, G. (1987). Male reference groups and discontent among female professionals. In B. Gutek and L. Larwood (eds) *Women's career development*, pp. 28–41. Newbury Park, CA: Sage.

Zanna, M. P. and Rempel, J. K. (1988). Attitudes: A new look at an old concept. In D. Bar-Tal and A. Kruglanski (eds) *The social psychology of knowledge*, pp. 315–34. New York: Cambridge University Press.

Zillmann, D., Baron, R. A. and Tamborini, R. (1981). Social costs of smoking: Effects of tobacco smoke on hostile behavior. *Journal of Applied Social Psychology*, 11, 548–61.

INDEX

GROUP PROCESS, GROUP DECISION, GROUP ACTION
Robert S. Baron, Norbert L. Kerr and Norman Miller

Groups are a key part of human experience. Whether the group is a family, a street gang, a work group, an ethnic minority or a network of friends, group membership and influence represents one of the most powerful forces shaping our feelings, judgments and behaviours. While group processes can lead to aggressive and destructive outbursts, so too are they a source of love, achievement, nurturance, loyalty and sacrifice. In this book the authors share the excitement and challenge of conducting research on groups. They familiarize the reader with the theoretical perspectives and data that provide us with the means of interpreting group phenomena. They place special emphasis on several aspects of group experience that they feel are particularly significant: social influence, group productivity, group decision-making, and intergroup conflict and prejudice; and they explore the significance for and application of group theory in our everyday lives.

... this book is carefully formulated and presents a good source of information for those interested in group dynamics and social psychology in general.

(*Newsletter of the Open University Psychological Society*)

Contents
Introduction – Social facilitation – Individual versus group performance – Group motivation losses – Social influence and conformity – Group decision making – Social dilemmas – Group aggression and intergroup conflict – Stress and social support – Crowding – Concluding thoughts – References – Index.

256pp   0 335 09862 2 (Paperback)

SOCIAL PSYCHOLOGY AND HEALTH
Wolfgang Stroebe and Margaret S. Stroebe

This book discusses major topics of health psychology from a social psychological perspective. This approach reflects the significant changes which have taken place in conceptions of health and illness during recent decades and the move away from purely biomedical models of illness. In line with this broadening perspective, health psychology has become a dominant force in the health sciences, a field to which social psychological theory and research has much to offer. The book addresses two major factors detrimental to health and well-being, namely health impairing behaviors and stressful life events. The following key questions are discussed: which behavior patterns are detrimental to one's health? Why do people engage in health impairing behaviors even if they know about their negative effects? How can people be influenced to change their behavior? What are stressful life events and which mechanisms mediate the impact of these stresses on health? The book argues for an integrative approach that combines psychological, economic and environmental interventions to reduce behavioral risk factors.

Contents
Changing conceptions of health and illness – Determinants of health behavior: a social psychological analysis – Beyond persuasion: the modification of health behavior – Behavior and health: excessive appetites – Behavior and health: self-protection – Stress and health – Moderators of the stress-health relationship – The role of social psychology in health – References – Author index – Subject index.

204pp   0 335 09857 6 (Paperback)   0 335 09858 4 (Hardback)